Endorsements

"Giving is a matter of both science and art. When it is done right, the world is a better place, and we know that we are part of that. Steve Perry's clear principles, moving stories and practical suggestions make this a must-read to expand our capacity. One of the highlights is that Steve uses actual case histories and real dollars in his narratives. This is such a benefit to the reader!"
Dr. John Townsend, New York Times bestselling author

Knowing Steve is like having a close friend whose possesses a bent sense of humor that always surprises you. Reading this book is like sitting in his living room having Steve regale with a grand story that compels you to be a better version of yourself. The Accidental Philanthropist is a penetratingly honest account of one family's growth to understand their calling and make a difference in managing the giving of significant resources. It is not just a peak behind the curtain of the impenetrable secrecy of most philanthropies, but a full-on tour of the what, where, when, why and how of generosity and wise stewardship. No matter the scope of the resources you are responsible for this is a must read for anyone wanting to be engaged in righteous philanthropy. And besides that, it is a great read.
Rob Martin, Partner, First Fruit Institute. Author, *"When Money Goes on Mission: Fundraising and Giving in the 21st Century"*

It's unusual to find a pastor who truly understands the blessings and challenges of wealth yet chooses not to preach about it. Steve Perry tells his personal story in a way that will encourage, inspire, and lead you into exploring your own unique journey.

Fred Smith, Founding President of The Gathering

For more than 35 years I have worked with families who have struggled with the responsibility of great wealth. I have found that their number one need is counsel and advice from someone who has personally faced the issues that come with financial prosperity. In this book, Steve Perry shares invaluable wisdom from God as he, and Susie, worked out their own journey of generosity. I highly recommend it to everyone who finds themselves on a similar journey.

Terry Parker, Co-Founder, National Christian Foundation

Over the last 25 years, I have witnessed Steve and Susie Perry's generous, sacrificial, and strategic giving to organizations with vision and purpose that bring hope and healing to a hurting world. They have changed lives by assisting college students, providing hospital care in developing countries, attending to orphans in South Africa, and blessing inner-city kids. These pages capture that wisdom and share lessons learned over a lifetime of generosity and faithfulness that can help shape our own giving practices.

David E. Bixby, Ed.D. Executive Vice President of Azusa Pacific University

Accidental Philanthropist

Steve Perry

with Steve Halliday

Accidental Philanthropist
A Journey Toward Intentional Generosity

Copyright 2019 by Steven Perry

ISBN 978-0-5782-2466-4

Dedication

Plans fail for lack of counsel, but with many advisers they succeed.

PROVERBS 15:22

If you want to go fast, you go it alone. If you want to go far, you go together.

AFRICAN PROVERB

None of us ever succeeds solely by ourselves.

Throughout our fifteen years of leading a foundation, my wife, Susie, and I have leaned upon the assistance, skills and counsel of our board members and staff. Sacred Harvest would not be where it is today without the trusted guidance, talents and godly counsel of these men and women. Nor could we come this far without the support and encouragement of these individuals who believe in our mission. We have come further than we ever dreamed or imagined fifteen years ago because of these men and women.

Board Members	Advisory Board Members
Brett Trowbridge	Matt and Kate Perry
Glenn Parrish	Jenny and Ryan Somers
David Worland	
Terry Parker	
Kelly Sheperd	

Orange County-based Staff	Philippines-based Staff	Maui-based Staff
Steve Komanapalli	Josefa Bautista	David Allaire
David Holden	Joel Pranza	
Jill Tilk	Rafunzel Pabunag	
Tasha Iglesias	Tweela Praise Gacal	
Kristy Martin	Precious Pabalate	
Tom Miller	Germae Urbiztondo	

Our humblest and deepest thanks and appreciation to each and every one of these for our journey together.

Steve and Susie Perry

Table of Contents

Introduction

Who Wants to Be a Philanthropist?

Probably no one in history has ever arrived on this planet with a desire to become a philanthropist. If you ask any ten-year-old whether he or she dreams of doing philanthropy, I'll bet 99.9 percent will say," no"—or at best, "what's that?"

When my wife, Susie, and I first met during our senior year at Azusa Pacific University in 1974, my spiritual piety demanded that I vigorously pursue "non-wealth." Because I considered money to be spiritual poison, the only right thing to do with it was to give it away. Susie, on the other hand, had grown up in a farming family in Orange County, California. Throughout her childhood, the family resembled most farming families: dirt rich, cash poor. Neither her parents nor her grandparents bequeathed to Susie a vision about becoming a philanthropist.

All of that changed in 1965 when the state of California decided to run the 405 Freeway through the middle of the family's farm. Suddenly, her parents found themselves faced with new realities that promised far more productivity than tilling dirt. Soon they got into property development and began building their biggest and most valuable project, South Coast Plaza, now considered a mega shopping complex.

When Susie and I married, I had to come to grips with my "spiritual poison" attitude toward money. That adjustment took a long time. In my first book, *Living with Wealth Without Losing Your Soul,* I explained how God dealt with me and changed my outlook about financial blessings and responsibility. In the pages that follow, I hope to offer some advice, counsel and hard-won insight into how to become intentionally generous.

Those who, like me, have enjoyed unexpected or unplanned good fortune usually find themselves facing hard questions about how to live with such uncommon wealth. Susie and I allowed our Christian faith to inform our response. We have always believed that as children of God, we are "blessed to be a blessing," no matter the size of our wealth. That principle, so deeply embedded in our DNA, raised vital questions for us when the family business became a tremendous financial success. How could we use this unexpected blessing from God to be a blessing to others?

Please do not imagine, however, that becoming intentionally generous was a slam dunk for us! It wasn't—as you will soon see. Also, please do not assume that having wealth automatically makes anyone generous. I learned long ago that wealth, like fame, merely magnifies who you already are. Though we viewed wealth as a blessing, we discovered that it also greatly magnified our imperfections. Our financial blessings led to moments of great stress and debate over how we should use that wealth to bless others.

What's Ahead

If you are reading this book because you want to use some of your resources to make a positive difference in this world, you should first recognize that having wealth does not necessarily mean you will live generously, regardless of your intent. I have seen poor individuals acting in extremely generous ways despite their meager resources, and I've observed wealthy individuals appearing reluctant to part with a single dollar. I have also observed poor people consumed with materialism, and rich folks passionate about fulfilling their "mission" to share their wealth.

Please understand: I have no intention of lecturing the wealthy for their avarice or praising the poor for their virtue. I have come to believe that, while those who have enjoyed tremendous blessings often have a desire to give generously of their wealth, they often fail to become as big-hearted as they really want to be.

Why does this so often happen? First, these generous individuals face obstacles that have nothing to do with greed, but rather, with the realities of life. Second, they lack a strategy for their generosity. I will talk at length about both factors in Part Two of this book, *Anyone's Journey*.

In Part One, *The Sacred Harvest Journey*, I'd like to sketch out for you the path we've taken, to give you some context for figuring out where you want to go. I do not describe our journey to suggest you should travel the same path, for you should design your own. And so, in Part Three, *Your Journey*, I will suggest several critical factors to ponder as you plan your own journey toward smarter generosity.

Intentional generosity—the kind that does real good in this world—must become deeply thoughtful. Merely reactive generosity cannot consistently achieve our goals. Of course, occasions may arise when some critical need confronts us and we react; however, if all our giving merely responds to the events thrust upon us or the people we happen to meet, we will give only in a measured way, never generously.

In *Accidental Philanthropist*, I will highlight many of the steps that our family took over a fifteen-year period, hoping that some of our experience will help you to proactively map your own path to becoming the generous person you want to be and the big-hearted person you have been naturally equipped to be.

But please remember this: every principle and experience relayed in this book developed out of what happened in *our* lives on *our* path. I include these stories and accounts only to help stimulate your thinking so that you can become more intentional (and I hope smarter!) —about how you steward the resources that have been entrusted to you.

Steve Perry
January 2019

Part One

The Sacred
Harvest Journey

Chapter One

The Early Years

From everyone to whom much has been given, much will be required.

JESUS

The day before Bill Gates married Melinda French in 1994, his mother, Mary, wrote a letter to her soon-to-be daughter-in-law.

"From those to whom much is given," the letter read, "much is expected."[1]

About six months later, Mary Gates passed away. And just a few months after her death, Bill Gates allocated around $100 million to what eventually would become the *Bill & Melinda Gates Foundation*, a charitable organization that today boasts an endowment worth over forty *billion* dollars.

That's a lot of giving! Do you think it began only after Bill's marriage? Surely not. After Melinda received that letter from his mother, however, it appears Bill's focus and attention began to change and sharpen. And fourteen years later in 2008, he left Microsoft to work fulltime as co-chair of the foundation.

When I see the progression of the Gates' philanthropy, I see faint echoes of the giving journey that Susie and I have taken. I am no Bill

Gates, of course! Still, the two of us do share a few similarities. For example, at the beginning, neither of us had a clear vision of how to do effective philanthropy. I doubt many of us do as we begin. Over time, both Bill and I also left our careers to focus on our giving and to encourage others to give generously. And eventually, both of us learned (as every philanthropist must) that effective giving takes intentionality and the willingness to share one's influence to encourage others to greater and more effective generosity.

All of us—whether Bill Gates, you or me—share at least one thing in common. Each of us has experienced a unique moment that pushed us to become more intentional with our giving or had a person of influence who stepped into our lives and helped crystalize that decision. Like Bill and Melinda Gates, many of us have parents who greatly inspired us toward lives of generosity. Others of us got a wake-up call from peers, perhaps like Warren Buffet's "Billionaire Challenge" to give away half one's wealth to good causes. Still others begin a life of philanthropy out of a deepening sense of social responsibility or the need to "pay back," very often as a result of a financial windfall. For individuals such as ourselves and many of our friends, the motivation to greater giving grows out of a profound experience of faith (more on the motivations for giving in Chapter 12). Once that decision is made, however, a host of questions begin to rise up, and none of them have easy answers:

> All of us share at least one thing in common. Each of us has experienced a unique moment that pushed us to become more intentional with our giving or had a person of influence who stepped into our lives and helped crystalize that decision.

- ➤ How much should we give?
- ➤ Shall we give out of our income or our assets?
- ➤ How does this affect our estate plan?
- ➤ How much do we leave to charity and how much to our family?

Probably of greatest importance and interest is this question: Where and to whom shall we give?

Susie and I have had to wrestle with all these questions, and more. At first, we utterly failed to take into account our radically different perspectives and approaches to life. That very concern would become our first and greatest struggle in our own journey to wiser and more intentional generosity.

Hunter vs. Nester

God has blessed us to be a blessing; both Susie and I have always believed that. But like many couples, we often have *very* different philosophies about how to manage our money.

Sociologists might refer to me as a "hunter," or to use today's preferred term, a "pioneer." I like living on the edge! I hardly ever stop to think about matters of financial security. Susie, on the other hand, is a "nester" or "settler." She loves security and definitely wants to know what she can afford today as well as for the long-term future.

Strangely, our biggest conflicts never erupted over how we spent our money, but over how much we gave. When Susie would receive her quarterly distributions from the family business, I felt it imperative that we immediately make our financial gifts and grants. If we didn't, I worried that we would forget to give at all. The nester in Susie would get upset and say, "Can't I at least hold it in my hand for a little while?"

Inevitably a debate would ensue. "If we don't give it now," I would insist, "we will forget about it." (Can you detect my voice growing louder?)

Driven by my fear of us failing in our commitment to grow generously, I invariably became condescending of Susie's concern, and resorted to an old preachers story.

A man had faithfully tithed his whole life. He gave to the Lord ten percent of what he earned, no matter how much he made. When he made fifty dollars, he gave five dollars. When he made one hundred dollars, he gave ten. As the years went by, his business grew and when he began making $5,000 a week, every Sunday he wrote a $500 check to his church. After a while, he began to think, *That's a lot of money to be giving away.* It troubled him. While he didn't want to stop tithing, he could not stop thinking of the ton of money he gave away every week. One day he decided to speak with his pastor about it.

"Pastor," he said, "I have been a faithful tither my whole life, and I don't want to stop being one. But, wow—giving $500 a week? That is a lot of money to be giving away! I don't know what to do."

The pastor put his hand on the man's shoulder and kindly said, "Let's pray about it. 'Lord,'" the pastor began, "this man has indeed been faithful to give 10% of his income to your work. And he wants to remain faithful to his commitment. But now, he feels that he is giving way too much. So, I humbly ask, would you please lower his income so that he is no longer troubled?"

We all know what usually occurs when we try to apply cold logic to an emotional subject. My story did little more than irritate Susie and made me sound patronizing. I recognized that if we were to move forward, we would need to find a way to overcome both her fears and my rigidity. We needed a plan that could satisfy her nester instincts and my overwhelming sense of obligation. Only in that way could we become the generous people we were created to be.

Simple Solutions

As Susie and I discussed our problem, we developed a couple of solutions that began working really well for us. Together, these plans put us on a journey toward being more intentional.

Make the nest bigger. First, we simply made Susie's nest larger. We decided to build up her household checking account to cover about six months' worth of expenses, rather than try to maximize returns by putting away as much as possible in a higher interest-bearing account. We recognized that Susie's nesting instincts was limiting her ability to understand how much money we actually had once it was invested. When the funds went out of sight, they also went out of her mind: the money ceased to exist in my wife's consciousness. To Susie, our financial capability as a family was constrained by what she could see in our household checking account.

> The Charity Checkbook reminded us that this money would serve only one purpose.

So, by keeping a balance in her checking account of half a year's worth of expenses, we alleviated her fears about tomorrow.

The Charity Checkbook. Susie and I instituted what we called the Charity Checkbook, nothing more than a second checking account for the sole purpose of storing our tithes and offerings until we were ready to give them. By using this simple system, our giving began operating like a line item in our budget, with its own set of records and accounting. The Charity Checkbook reminded us that this money would serve only one purpose.

The Charity Checkbook created a valuable side benefit as well: we soon found it easy to track our gifts for tax purposes. No longer did we have to scour through page after page of check registries or bank statements to find our charitable donations.

Even as we fulfilled our charitable commitments through our Charity Checkbook, we also held back a percentage to maintain a reserve that gave us the ability to respond to unforeseen opportunities. Perhaps we had in mind Galatians 6:10, which says, "Therefore, as we have opportunity, let us do good to all people, especially to those who belong to the family of believers" (NIV).

At the beginning of each year, we would agree on what percentage of our income to put into our charity account. We challenged ourselves to increase that percentage by at least 1 percent each year. While the tithe from my paycheck went to our church, our tithes and offerings from the family's business distributions went into the charity account for broader giving to other organizations as well. We often also gave funds from the charity account to our church for special projects or events outside of the church's regular operating budget.

The Result

To my great surprise, this simple but more disciplined practice *worked*. The stress and debate over our giving virtually disappeared. But why?

As a nester, Susie could still see where our money was. As a hunter, I no longer feared we would forget our commitments to give. We didn't have to rush to give it away, and most importantly, we didn't take our charitable giving out of my wife's household checking account.

Once we started down this path, I watched as Susie began to grow more and more generous. By that point in our marriage, we had committed to giving away fifteen percent of our income. One day, Susie told me that she had deposited a quarterly distribution from the family business. With all the fortitude of an inquisitor, I asked, "Did you make the deposit into the Charity Checkbook?"

"Yes," she replied.

"Well, did you put in the amount we had agreed upon?"

"Yes," she replied, and then told me the amount she had deposited: 20 percent instead of 15 percent! Part of the inquisitor in me died that day.

Thank God.

The Next Development

A few short years after starting the Charity Checkbook, our business distributions began to increase sharply. Very quickly, our capacity to give truly exceeded our vision to give.

At the same time, we recognized a significant problem with the Charity Checkbook: it was not a tax-deductible organization. You might ask, "Why should that be a problem? Don't statistics state that the primary motivator for people's giving is *not* a charitable tax deduction, whether they're religious or not?" Neither was that our primary motivator.

But the government has long insisted that a percentage of one's income and estate belongs to the wellbeing of society. The state therefore gives you and me an option regarding how we choose to invest in society's wellbeing: we can

> "From those to whom much is given, much is expected."

do so either through taxes or charitable giving. To encourage the latter, the government allows a tax deduction for gifts given to government-recognized charities, often referred to as 501(c)(3) nonprofit organizations (the designation comes from the portion of the U.S. tax code that describes tax-exempt groups considered public charities, private foundations or private operating foundations).

In this way, when you give a gift and take advantage of the allowed tax deduction, the government participates with you in supporting your favorite charity, thus leveraging your gift.

Privilege and Responsibility

I see philanthropy and generous giving as both a great privilege and a very real responsibility. I can't forget what Jesus told his disciples: "From everyone to whom much has been given, much will be *required;* and from the one to whom much has been entrusted, even more will be demanded" (Luke 12:48, NRSV, emphasis added).

While I doubt that the world sees Bill Gates as a religious man, I know that he and his wife are regularly involved with a Roman Catholic congregation in Washington state. I don't know where his mother took inspiration for the letter she gave to Melinda the day before her son's wedding, but I do know that Gates has kept that letter to this day.

> *"From those to whom much is given, much is expected."*

While Susie and I received no letter like that on our wedding day back in 1975, we still think about those words—*often!* I suppose they form part of the motivation we have felt to get better and more effective at this huge challenge of becoming wiser and more intentional. There's a lot to learn!

Once you start working with tax-exempt organizations, you have embarked on a major escalation in your charitable giving. And so, to that part of our journey we now turn.

Chapter Two

The Learning Years

Acknowledging what you don't know is the dawning of wisdom.

CHARLES MUNGER

When beginning any new enterprise or activity—any place where I am not a seasoned veteran— my first rule is to acknowledge "I don't know what I don't know." When Susie and I first started Sacred Harvest, we realized that we had plenty of unknowns yet to uncover. We therefore heeded the ancient counsel, "Plans fail for lack of counsel, but with *many* advisers they succeed" (Proverbs 15:22, emphasis added).

Through our fifteen years with the foundation, we have sought out the assistance, skills and counsel of board members, staff and sometimes consultants. Sacred Harvest would not be where it is today without the guidance, talents and sound counsel of these men and women.

Even though we have surrounded ourselves with capable people, however, the first rule still applies. That's *especially* true when heading into a new region—in our case, the Philippines—or in starting new initiatives.

The Five-Year Rule

The years have taught me to pay attention to a principle that I call the Five-Year Rule. With any new initiative or enterprise, it generally takes about five years for the leader and organization to discover where the opportunities and obstacles lie, and then to implement and test the strategies and tactics that will enable them to reach their targets.

At the same time, no one ever achieves 100 percent certainty, because healthy leaders and organizations always question their strategies and test their assumptions. It's all about discovery.

The same reality holds true in the journey toward wise generosity. In our case, building the "bigger nest" and Charity Checkbook strategies worked well for some time. But as the distributions from Susie's family business grew and our needs changed, we went in search of a new solution. Could *something* enable us to get a tax deduction, while allowing us to warehouse our charitable dollars until we could figure out where and when to invest them? Since we didn't know what we didn't know, we set out to find answers.

> ... healthy leaders and organizations always question their strategies and test their assumptions. It's all about discovery.

Most people know about the private foundation option, but the legal and accounting fees of setting up and running a private foundation are relatively large. We found a more convenient, simpler and, cheaper alternative: the donor-advised fund (see *Popular Giving Vehicles* in appendix).

The Donor Advised Fund

A Donor Advised Fund (DAF) looked like a perfect solution for us. We opened a DAF—also called a Giving Fund—at the National Christian Foundation (NCF). This organization strongly resembles the long-standing community foundations that have served local and religious communities for almost a century. The DAF accomplished far more than we could ever imagine. It functioned a lot like our Charity Checkbook, but with much less administration.

Since the community foundation is a public charity, we didn't have to save all the gift receipts for each donation we made to every charity. The foundation took care of all of that.

Once we made a gift to our DAF/GF, we also faced no time pressure to distribute the funds. The beauty of this system is well-illustrated by a friend who sometimes received a big bonus from his company at the end of the year. Whenever that happened, he had to spend the last few days of the year making gifts to various charities in order to take advantage of the tax deductions for that year. Trying to beat the end-of-year deadline often forced him to write a flurry of checks, devouring the time he needed for careful and thoughtful review.

I suggested that he simply write one check to his DAF/GF. He would then receive the benefit of the tax deduction for the appropriate year, and since the foundation applied no time pressure to give those funds to his chosen charities, he could be more thoughtful about how he invested his charitable dollars.

Such a foundation also handles all administrative details, such as mailing the grants, writing gift receipts and filing the annual 990 form with the IRS. Most institutions that offer DAF/GFs have online access where grant requests can be made 24/7. For most people, a DAF/GF is sufficient. The foundation becomes a good "back office" for all kinds of granting purposes.

The other great advantage of the DAF/GF is that it affords the opportunity to stay below the radar. A DAF/GF requires no individual filing of an IRS Form 990, as with a private foundation, which reveals one's charitable assets and granting preferences. Instead, those assets and preferences lie buried within the community foundation's 990, which means pesky grant writers who cull 990s for potential grantors can never find you. Our DAF gave us the ability to remain anonymous whenever we wanted to work unnoticed. At the same time, we could request that a grant go out without our names attached. (As a grantor, sometimes you want to support a good work—and you also don't want to land on yet another mailing list!)

One word of caution: Before you begin utilizing a community foundation, or one housed within a big financial house, confirm its willingness to grant funds to the charities you want to support. By law, the foundation has the right to approve or not approve your grant request. Because the boards of these foundations rotate over the years, charities once viewed as favorable can fall out of favor. A case in point: an individual who for years had ardently supported the Boy Scouts through his community foundation discovered that the Boy Scouts had fallen out of favor with the board. The foundation would no longer approve any grants to that organization.

Every institution that offers DAFs must define what it will or will not support. The IRS has ruled that when a donation is made, the donor relinquishes control of the gift; otherwise, it cannot be considered a genuine gift. Be sure to ask whether the charities or types of charities you are considering will or will not receive support from the community foundation. We live in a time of shifting cultural norms, so, to avoid any surprises, obtain a signed agreement that your DAF will continue to approve grants to the charities or types of charities that you choose to support.

As time rolls on, the day may come when the asset base of your DAF/GF grows to such an extent that you need to travel and hire staff or consultants in order to do your due diligence for granting purposes. This happened to us. Many people in this situation go the private foundation (PF) route, without realizing its limitations on tax deductions for contributions of cash and appreciated assets. A PF also lacks anonymity, due the annual filing of the IRS's 990, which becomes part of the public record. We therefore chose a different route.

The Supporting Organization

In 2003, through the services of the NCF, we were introduced to another giving option that better suited our needs: the Supporting Organization (SO).

The SO is probably the least recognized and understood of the three IRS-approved giving entities. Classified as a public charity, it provides donors with higher limits on their charitable tax deductions than does a PF. Unlike PF's, it has no 2 percent tax on earned income and no 5 percent minimum distribution rule if you want to endow your SO. It also affords donors the anonymity they often desire, as well as allowing them to hire staff.

The only downside for many people is that donors cannot maintain majority control over the SO's granting authority. A board is required, with representation from the Supported Organization. In our case, this meant the NCF.

Susie and I were given the choice of three non-family board members, one of them a representative of NCF. Since we knew several of the NCF staff, we had the freedom to choose our NCF representative. We individually wrote down the three people who we wanted to make up our board, and to our great delight, we discovered both of us had written down the same three names.

While some might consider this board requirement a disadvantage, we found it to be highly beneficial. The other three members of our board consisted of long-time, trusted friends who brought a wealth of added skills and experience that we did not possess.

When people begin to be intentional about their charitable giving, one strength they usually lack is clarity of purpose and passion. As we began this new leg of our charitable journey, our new board guided us through a process to help us develop our initial "mission, vision, and values" statements. During a two-day retreat, we arrived at a philosophical position that, surprisingly, has changed very little over fifteen years. What *has* changed is a greater clarity in our mission and vision, and a reaffirmation of our values.

Another value in having a board is knowing that if something were to happen to me, my wife and children will have trusted friends to assist them in continuing the work of the Sacred Harvest Foundation.

Of course, no one needs an SO to have a board. Many functioning family boards are often augmented with wise friends and advisors, although the government does not require such groups to have such boards. But ask yourself this: if having a board of advisors is good (although not required) for business, then why would it not also be good for one's charitable business?

With the SO, we gained the ability to hire staff and consultants, as well as cover the foundation's operating expenses. Today, we have two fulltime and one part time staff in Orange County, six fulltime in the Philippines, and one part time in Maui.

Would a private foundation have given us the same options? Yes, but since an SO is a public charity and not a private one, it offers greater benefits than does a private foundation. Because all our donations to Sacred Harvest come in the form of cash, with an SO, I can deduct up to 50 percent of my gross income. A private foundation, by contrast, allows a deduction of only 30 percent. Susie owns a lot of real estate and corporate interest, and with our SO (because it's a public charity), any donations we make in the form of non-liquid assets receive a tax deduction for fair market value. With a private foundation, donating non-liquid assets receives a deduction based only on the actual cost. These advantages also apply to the DAF/GF.

What to Fund?

The benefit of having a board and hiring staff and consultants has greatly accelerated our journey toward smarter philanthropy. The experience has taught us, for one thing, that we should not have a lot of preconceived notions about how we're going to "change the world."

Remember my first rule? I don't know what I don't know.

And neither do you.

I've learned, for example, that it's vital to meet in person the people we're considering for a grant, and we must meet them as close to "their" space as we can get. We can't always find out what we need to know from a document or a video. I've discovered that a site visit tends to be crucial in order to make a genuine, relational connection that helps us to truly understand both the organization and its leadership. (More on that later).

None of us know what we don't know. As you begin your own journey toward wiser and more intentional generosity, you'll need to have your own conversations to find your own path.

In the next chapter, I'll outline for you some of the key principles we've learned at Sacred Harvest about what it means to be intentional stewards of the resources entrusted to us. You will need to learn your own lessons, of course—but, just maybe, you can find some benefit in the insights we've gleaned over the past fifteen years.

Chapter 3

The Sacred Harvest Way

There are no shortcuts to any place worth going.

BEVERLY SILLS

Many successful companies employ the practice of "benchmarking" to improve the way they do business. These organizations compare the quality of their policies, products, programs and strategies against those used by other companies. Their purpose is to: (1) determine what and where improvements are needed, (2) analyze how other organizations achieve high levels of performance, and (3) improve their company's performance.[2]

This chapter will offer some depth about how Sacred Harvest "does business." Our purpose is not to convince you to do things our way, but to help stimulate your thinking about how to better find your own path. What works for us may not work for you at all, but I hope that some of the insights we've gleaned over the years may help you to accomplish your own mission even more effectively.

Five Guiding Principles

Five key themes consistently characterize how we choose what organizations to support and which projects to fund. We landed on each of these themes through a combination of intuition, trial and error, personal preference, and even theological conviction. Today these themes guide both how we operate and how we function. They have become our guiding principles.

1. Relational vs Institutional

Because I am an extrovert who pastored congregations for seventeen years, you might conclude that being "relational" expresses who I am as a leader more than it conveys any organizational strategic approach. True enough—but it also summarizes how I see ministry, and ministry for me *always* begins with the relational aspect. That goes equally for how I understand and approach grant-making.

At Sacred Harvest, we focus on helping leaders flourish in their calling; therefore, we strive to develop and maintain a healthy relationship with the leaders and organizations that we consider to be our core partners. Developing such relationships creates a bond of trust that allows them to speak freely to us regarding their issues and concerns, and vice versa.

Not long ago, one of our long-time partners (of two decades) conducted a feasibility study for a $3 million campaign. It had asked us to make the lead gift, but the feasibility study revealed that great confusion existed among its donor base regarding the organization's purpose and mission. Rather than hide this fact from us, the group's leaders admitted their great weakness in effectively communicating who they are and what they are about. Because we have partnered with them for so long, we knew their work had tremendous impact. We also highly valued this leadership team. Their admission did not cause us great fear and concern; on the contrary, we welcomed their transparency and honesty.

We have an odd saying in our office: "Bad news is good news." Because we tend to fund organizations of under $2 million, we expect opportunities for learning and growth. Who can grow without becoming aware of their weaknesses and shortcomings? Think of it like a trip to the doctor: do you want her to tell you only what you want to hear, or does she tell you the truth so you can get better? Until you can name the source of your pain, you can't get well. As a grantor, you cannot effectively know both the strengths and weaknesses of your grantees if your relationship lacks mutual trust and transparency. Many times, we have adjusted a grant proposal to address what a partner needed, rather than merely what it wanted.

Because we value being a relational donor over an institutional one, members of our staff often serve as mentors, coaches or friends to leadership teams. Over the past fifteen years, we have regularly heard leaders say, "it's lonely at the top." Leaders often have no safe place where they can admit their problems, either professionally or personally. They doubt they can talk to their staff about these issues and they often fear to speak to their board members. So, where can they turn? We want to be such a resource.

> "Sacred Harvest is a safe place for me."

At times, I've wondered if our relational approach has offered any concrete benefit to our partners. I received my answer at a recent lunch. As a ministry partner thanked me and the Sacred Harvest staff for our support and encouragement, he declared, "Sacred Harvest is a safe place for me."

Amen, I thought. That simple statement made all our efforts feel worthwhile.

2. *Slower over faster*

This principle comes out of the five-year rule I have already mentioned. A Master of Divinity degree does not necessarily equip anyone with great strategic or operational awareness! For the seventeen years that I pastored congregations, I functioned a lot out of trial-and-error or by mimicking other pastors. I learned quickly that launching a new initiative too quickly—motivated more by enthusiasm and good intentions than by careful forethought—rarely produced the results I wanted. In fact, usually I had to restart and get the fundamentals right. I often failed to fully appreciate the developmental process required when trying to build something new.

When Chip Kelly joined the Oregon Ducks football team in 2007 as offensive coordinator, the team had been struggling to achieve its potential. None of the traditional mantras had worked. Win the national championship? Win the Rose Bowl? Beat your greatest rivals? All great visions, but none of them achieved anything.

Needing a way to galvanize the team, in March 2007 the coaches held a brainstorming session. Coaches convened with players, equipment managers and trainers, trying to find solutions for the Ducks' malaise. Players yelled at players. Players yelled at coaches. Coaches yelled back. No one seemed to know what to do.

"We were terminal—the whole team," said John Neal, the defensive backs coach in 2007. Then the new offensive coordinator, Chip Kelly, asked this key question: "Why don't we just 'win the day'?"

The bickering stopped, and *Win the Day* quickly became the team's new motto. At each practice, everyone focused on each day's fundamentals in preparation for that week's game. Eventually the tactic helped turn the Ducks into a national powerhouse.[3]

So many of us as leaders and boards run into the same problem that stymied the Ducks: we get so caught up with the vision and the future that we don't take the time to learn and master the fundamentals necessary to get us where we need to go *today*.

When Sacred Harvest decided to launch a new training program called the Organizational Health Pathway (OHP) to help build capability and competency in Filipino and Orange County non-profit leaders, I told my team to go "low and slow." Despite the great skills and high competence of my team, none of us had real expertise in non-profit organizational development. How foolish to design a training process based on the vacuum of our own limited understanding! If we did not find effective ways to embrace the respective cultures we wanted to serve, we would design something contextually irrelevant to their needs and issues.

One of the great mistakes of philanthropy is to assume we fully understand the needs of those we desire to serve. Through the hard work and assistance of our staff, both in Orange County and in the Philippines, and with strong coaching from consultants in the field of organizational leadership, we created our beta model. For two years we field-tested it with three ministries in Orange County and five in Philippines. Boy, did we learn! We cut out 20 percent of our material, reorganized our presentations, re-contextualized our content for various cultures, re-did our assessment piece, and restructured our database to get the information we valued the most. Only then did we feel confident in declaring to the world that OHP could enhance an organization's impact and efficiency.

> One of the great mistakes of philanthropy is to assume we fully understand the needs of those we desire to serve.

Too often in our entrepreneurial society, we tend to think that a great vision and strategy guarantee a successful launch. We often forget that the success of any new enterprise also requires *time*. Any good business plan needs time to test its assumptions and to adequately develop its strategies. The old expression, "haste makes waste," holds as true today as ever.

Our willingness to go slowly gives us the time to engage with our third guiding principle.

3. Deeper over Wider

By moving slowly, we can go deeper with organizations, regions and leaders—which we believe will provide a greater impact. There are no short cuts to achieving personal and organization transformation! Success requires a presence both endearing (encouraging and supportive) and enduring (long and deep).

When my board realized that our international portfolio of grant-making made up only about 5 percent of our total budget, they kindly and astutely reminded Susie and me that the Bible says, "God so loved *the world*," not just the USA. Convicted by their words, we explored with them how to better address international concerns. "Do you want to fund opportunistic ventures that align with your vision and values, wherever they may appear around the world," they asked, "or do you want to focus on a particular region of the world and go deep and long?"

We chose the latter. If we were to achieve any meaningful impact, we knew we had to go deep and long, wherever we went. We eventually chose to venture into Mindanao, Philippines. Because we knew very little about the Philippines (remember, "we don't know what we don't know"), we hired a consulting firm to assist us in establishing our presence. The firm hired a program officer who could begin to vet appropriate partners and opportunities. At first, the people and ministry leaders in Mindanao expressed suspicion of us: "Who are you? Why are you here?" We eventually discovered that many well-intentioned organizations and foundations had come to the Philippines, only to pull out three years later. They left a bad taste in the mouth of many Filipinos, along with a lot of unfinished work.

We began our investment in the Philippines thirteen years ago and, throughout that time, we have focused on deepening relationships with our Filipino partners. By offering training opportunities through OHP, Church Health Pathway (CHP), Mission Increase Foundation (MIF), and by sponsoring Leadership Retreats and Missionary Care Retreats, we are no longer considered merely a grant-making institution. Our Filipino co-workers now consider us to be a trusted friend and partner.

Last year, a long-term U.S. ministry partner approached us for advice. It operates a school that transforms the lives of students who can't effectively learn or thrive in the school district's special education programs. This school provides students and their families the individual support and care required to help them learn and grow. I have firsthand knowledge of the school's effectiveness because my great nephew flourished under its tutelage. Parents often say, "This school has given us our lives back." These moms and dads beam as their once-troubled children become responsive, due to the love and encouragement received from a devoted staff. As one of their long-term partners, they trust us—and so they risked telling us at the meeting that they might have to close the school. They didn't know how they could make it through the summer and hoped we could help.

We recognized that every year they seemed to run short of funds, and we suspected the problem went beyond mere finances. With their permission, I asked my director to have an honest conversation with their board and director. He also participated in private meetings, attended board meetings, and brought in consultants and other resource partners. We wanted to understand, without judgment, what was really happening.

Within a few months, my director went back to the organization's board with a list of observations that we thought needed to be addressed. The two greatest changes involved the founder and the board living up to their duties and responsibilities. Even though we didn't have a pleasant conversation, they agreed (to our delight) with our list of concerns. Although we loved the original vision of the founder and the board—many struggling families considered it a lifeline—some areas needed to change. Organizations don't get started without a visionary, but that same person is not always the best suited to guide the enterprise forward to a place of stability or growth.

We said we would fund the organization to get it through the summer, if they would consider these changes. They began by hiring a new director/principal. The board added some new members while others left, and the school finally enlisted the parents of the students to help solve the funding problem. They promptly began networking with friends to increase enrollment.

While writing this book, I received a report from the group's new director and chairman of the board, after they had invested nine months in making needed changes. The board is taking ownership of the school by controlling the budget and raising funds. Parents have helped financially by using social media to tell family and friends how the school has transformed their children's learning and improved family dynamics. The school finished the year in the black, and enrollment for next year already has increased by 50 percent!

I must admit: our role in all this scared me. If our efforts had failed, Sacred Harvest would have become fodder for all those stories about over-controlling funders. But because we had invested hundreds of thousands of dollars through the years to support this awesome ministry, we felt we had a stewardship responsibility—not just to protect our investment, but to help ensure that a good and beneficial work continued for years to come.

4. Longer haul over quick fix

On average, we have worked with each of our Core Partners more than ten years, mainly because we began supporting some of them before we formed Sacred Harvest fifteen years ago. We prefer the longer haul over the quick fix.

Frankly, there are as many good arguments against this strategy as for it. Here's the main one: don't build dependency (we'll talk more about this in chapter 8, "Do No Harm"). Also, when you terminate a long-term grant, you always get an uncomfortable feeling about it. I know that firsthand, and maybe you do, too. You can avoid that dependency by making sure that the organization does not *count* on your funding for its existence. We try to stay under 10 percent of a group's operational budget. In case you must ever choose to discontinue your support, your decision will not sink the organization.

We think the benefits of such a strategy outweigh the disadvantages. When we started Sacred Harvest, I wanted to help organizations achieve sustainability, in part by choosing to support the group's operational fund. After about seven years, that conviction began to wane, and I began wondering how we might exit from some of our long-term partnerships. My board, which often has the collective memory of an elephant, reminded me of my own words (don't you hate that?) and forced me to rethink my plan. We never went through with those exit strategies, although we have cut ties with a couple of groups.

The greatest benefit of having a long-term commitment to a region or organization is the amount of influence you may accrue. An old saying in the church goes, "people don't care how much you know until they know how much you care." When you invest *time* in building a healthy relationship, you often get the amazing opportunity to speak into the life of a leader or the experience of an organization.

In 2014, we held an open house in Davao, Mindanao, to announce the launch of our OHP training. One hundred and twenty-two people showed up! Although I assumed this might be normal, one of our Filipino friends whispered to me, "All these people are here because Sacred Harvest has had a presence in Mindanao for seven years. They trust you."

Of course, we want our partners to go wider. We want to help them achieve greater reach and impact. But that "wide-ness" usually takes time.

When leaders from International Care Ministries (ICM) saw our Church Health Pathway, they asked us to help them train their pastors. ICM has a serious mission to reach the ultra-poor. For the last quarter of a century, it has achieved success by developing house churches, where pastors promote holistic transformation in their small communities through effective livelihood practices, proper health care, and values formation. We agreed to help, and so for two years our teaching staff trained ten pastor trainers from ICM, who in turn trained more than 1000 pastors. During those two years, our team worked with each of the ten trainers through a weekly encouraging email and video, a monthly video mentoring call and a quarterly three-day training from our teaching staff. The length and depth of our investment with these ten trainers resulted in over 19,300 people placing their faith in Christ and over 9,100 baptisms!

We believe that by taking the long view to mentor and coach, we can better equip leaders to handle the responsibilities they face. For this reason, each of our two key trainings—Organizational Health Pathway and Church Health Pathway—involve two years of training and coaching. We also remain available long after the training process ends.

Growth and maturation rates differ among all people and organizational systems. Because growth is such an organic process, you can't prescribe it ahead of time. Consequently, we willingly commit the appropriate time necessary so that both the leader and organization can flourish in their calling.

5. Better over Bigger

Bigger is *not* always better, nor is smaller always better. *Better* is better.

Sometimes, the heart and soul of a ministry rests in an individual more than it does in the organization. And how do you clone that person's passion, insight and commitment? You can't. Trying to expand it by using previous mechanisms won't work. You'll either kill the new person or the effort will just fail. Doubling an organization won't necessarily get you double the impact . . . as I have seen in the restaurant industry.

Better is better.

My wife's family has worked as landlords in the retail industry for fifty years. They have learned that expansion can kill great restaurants. They have seen many successful eating establishments die as a result of trying to increase their size. Too late they learned that growth in sales does not always keep pace with higher rent.

In a similar way, some small non-profits are perfect just as they are. They provide a good, manageable service, and any misguided attempt at expansion can overload their ability. Yet the idea of getting bigger and faster engulfs many non-profits. What often happens? In their pursuit of greater size and larger numbers, they compromise their ability to serve effectively while remaining financially sustainable. Scale *always* comes at a risk.

We like to say, "Make sure you're doing the right things, and make sure you're doing them well." Doing a lot of things doesn't necessarily mean doing the right things (and certainly not doing the best things). Non-profits need to make sure they're doing the right things in the best way they know how. Why should we always shoot for doing things bigger? Life is developmental; you must invest time on the foundation before you can build the superstructure. While numbers are important, at the end of the day, if quality or capability gets compromised, what was the point?

When we think of "better," we have health in mind. We like to use the words "health" or "flourish" rather than "growth." We assume that if a group is healthy, it will grow; if not in size, then definitely in impact. By seeking to help our leaders flourish in their calling, they'll have greater impact with those they serve, and we'll have a better return on our philanthropic investment.

> By seeking to help our leaders flourish in their calling, they'll have greater impact with those they serve, and we'll have a better return on our philanthropic investment.

A few years ago, one of our favorite partners in the Philippines came to us with a new grant request. The organization's board decided it wanted to expand the ministry into Indonesia. Don't all successful organizations expand? But as we looked at the previous year's budget, we saw it had a significant shortfall. We asked, "How can you even *think* about expanding operations when you can't support what you have going now?"

So, we gave them this counsel: "we love what you're doing, and we will give you a 'love gift' to help stabilize your ministry financially—but it is not to be used for expansion into Indonesia. We strongly encourage you to focus on getting healthy, not growing bigger." To our delight, they received our counsel and stopped operating on budgetary shortfalls that compromised their ability to serve.

Most of us don't often get to see another person or organization flourish. It just doesn't happen that frequently. If you were to ask our staff members where they get their greatest satisfaction, however, I think they'd all say, "from watching those we serve flourish in their calling." If you ever have the opportunity to use your time, talent and/or treasure to help a leader or organization flourish in their calling, you too may find it to be as addicting as we have.

Sacred Harvest's Seven-Layer Filter
In addition to the five guiding principles we use to determine where and how we might become involved in some new work, we also employ a seven-layer "filter" that gives us a foundational grid for everything we do. Here is a very brief look.

1. Scriptural foundation
As our name is *Sacred* Harvest, and we're currently led by a retired Lutheran pastor (me), you might guess that we take our marching orders from a higher authority. From the beginning, we've been guided by the Great Commission (Matthew 28:19-20) and the Great Commandment (Matthew 25:35-40).

2. Community collaboration
We love to leverage opportunities between civic, corporate and church entities.

3. Christ-like relation
We try to get alignment in relationships by being mutually accountable. We strive to do what we say we're going to do. We aim to deliver, every time. We refuse to take people for a ride.

4. Sustainable transformation

We stimulate ongoing change through a life-on-life process. *No transformation happens without the involvement of a community of people.* Any change has three core elements: God, community, and time.

5. Soul restoration

We work to reconcile lives and communities through *shalom*, the way God intended.

6. Foster rejuvenation

We help Christian leaders flourish in their God-given calling. We do not much care about the size of the ministry that we work with; we care very much that the ministry exhibits a desire and willingness to learn and become better and more efficient. This filter implies that the usual philanthropic notion of "best in class" often gets thrown out of an eight-story window.

7. Family dedication

We are dedicated to "family" in the larger sense, which demands generosity, humility and integrity.

By *generosity*, we mean that we want to encourage people to give what they have, whether a million dollars or ten bucks. A spirit of generosity has more to do with one's heart than one's resources. We want to inspire generous living more than merely generous giving.

By *humility*, we mean that we want to be just as honest about our weaknesses as we are about our strengths.

By *integrity*, we mean that we want a close correspondence between what we say and what we do.

Bottom Line: Value Investing

Since its inception, Sacred Harvest has invested over fifty million dollars in various organizations, both in the United States and around the world.

In many ways, what we do is like value investing. We look for leverage. We constantly ask where we can place our philanthropic crowbar to create the biggest impact. Sometimes this means we will take months to investigate an opportunity: we'll look at it this way and that way, ask more questions, and then look at it some more. We're searching for that crowbar.

A long-time friend founded a family ministry several years ago. His organization focuses on fostering "strong marriages, confident parents, and empowered kids" and exists to "strengthen and equip parents, couples and families." Back in the late nineties, this friend and I had a conversation about his group's difficulty in finding ways to fund itself. At the time, he ministered almost exclusively to youth and youth directors . . . people who had no money. The people *with* money who supported him did so because they loved him, not because they understood what he did.

"Look," I said to him, "the problem is that the people who have the money to support you are not experiencing what you're doing. They need to experience it. You need to hold a parents' retreat." I pledged to give him a small grant to fund it.

I have been told that the initial group of thirty couples who attended that retreat have since given his ministry over a million dollars. Why? Because they connected with him beyond the niceties of, "He's a great guy, trustworthy and a terrific leader." Once they began to experience what he was doing, the ministry took off. That's value investing!

We want to know: where can we get the most bang for the buck? Where can we apply significant leverage? How can we wisely invest to get an outsized influence on a significant problem?

We take great joy in growing our fruit on other people's trees—which seems only fitting for a guy who married a farmer's daughter and who with her started an organization called Sacred Harvest.

Part Two

Anyone's Journey

Chapter 4

Obstacles to Generosity

We have met the enemy and he is us.

POGO

A wealthy banker had never given any kind of donation to a particular local charity in his town, so one day the charity's director called the man. "Our records show you make half a million dollars a year," he said, "yet you haven't given a penny to charity. Wouldn't you like to help this community?"

The banker angrily replied, "Did your research also show that my mother is ill, with sky-high medical bills?"

"Um, no," mumbled the director.

"Or that my brother is blind and unemployed? Or that my sister's husband died, leaving her broke with four kids?"

"I … I … I had no idea."

"So," said the banker, "if I don't give *them* any money, why would I give any to *you*?"

For good reason someone once said, "When it comes to charity, most people stop at nothing." Jay Leno may have had that reality in mind when he asked, 'Why don't oysters give to charity?"

His answer: "because they're shellfish."

I must say, though, that I have met very few wealthy people who act like either the banker or the oyster. Most of the men and women of means whom I know really want to make a difference in their communities, states and world through their philanthropic giving. They're not shellfish, or any other kind of mollusk or crustacean. They truly want to help; they just haven't figured out how to get beyond the obstacles that keep them from becoming as generous as they'd like to be.

In our own journey toward smarter generosity, we've encountered several obstacles that we had to learn how to overcome. For us, these obstacles clustered in two main categories: *psychological* struggles and *practical* issues.

Psychological Struggles

Both guilt and fear play a role in the struggle many of us have in trying to discover how to live more generously. Although these forces act on us in different ways, they both prompt us to want to hide and withdraw.

Guilt

Most Americans have a hard time imagining the heavy guilt that individuals of means may feel over their wealth. I might even compare it to "survivor's guilt." Combat soldiers or survivors of cancer—people who have witnessed the deaths of many others—often have a question haunting their souls: *Why me? Why did I survive while all the others died?* For them, survival is a bittersweet reality. While they feel thankful that they lived, they also feel guilty that they somehow managed to "cheat death."

Wealthy people can suffer from a similar sense of guilt, especially in this age when many identify the "one percenter" as the enemy or the greedy. In such a society, strong feelings of guilt can easily get reinforced.

Unfortunately, an inability to fully embrace one's blessings severely hinders a person's ability to appreciate what he or she has been given.

And when you have trouble truly appreciating the bounty given to you, you also will likely have difficulty outwardly expressing your gratitude in thanksgiving and joy. Consider this: if you express how grateful you feel for your financial blessings, and someone rebukes you for saying so, how eager will you feel to publicly express your gratitude the next time?

Susie and I struggled with this issue. In the years when her family's business started earning ever larger returns, I pastored a church. How do you tell anyone in your congregation, "Rejoice with us, we just received a check for a million dollars"? You don't. Our inability to fully accept our blessings, without guilt or apology, not only muffled our ability to express our gratitude, it also deeply affected our ability to be truly generous.

Fears

Feelings of guilt over one's financial blessings can easily morph into another negative emotion, fear—especially the fear that others will judge you. Susie and I never wanted to be seen as "different" from others. But as soon as you get labeled "rich," suddenly you are *not* an "everyday person."

As Susie grew up, sometimes people would say to her, "It must be nice to be rich. Do you get to shop for free at South Coast Plaza?" Boys refused to ask her out because they perceived her as wealthy. She decided to attend college at Azusa Pacific University, about an hour's drive from her home, in part because very few there would likely know her maiden name, "Segerstrom." She could escape for a while from the notoriety she really didn't want.

We also discovered that some would judge us for merely *trying* to be generous. More than one person accused us of "showing off" when we gave a gift.

As I've said, in this era where class warfare seems to grow by the day, many wealthy people fear getting classified as a "one percenter." They try hard to hide their wealth, at least in certain environments (at church, for example). If you know you're going to get criticized for making a significant donation to some worthy charity, you may feel tempted to do nothing. You may choose to become a poster child for mollusks: You'll stop at nothing. At the very least, you'll minimize your response.

Protection Mechanisms

A different kind of emotion arose for us when we noticed others targeting us for our money. When you're wealthy, others--especially in the non-profit world--often seem to view you as an ATM machine. Many value you not as a person, but only for your net worth. As a result, they send a subliminal message, "You have money and I have need, so where is the problem?"

I recall a story of a typhoon that roared across the south Pacific. Within minutes, high waves swamped a beautiful yacht, sending it to the bottom without a trace.

The only two survivors—the boat's owner, Dr. Smith, and its steward, Reginald—both managed to swim to the closest island, a deserted little strip of mostly barren rock. Reginald began to weep, sobbing that no one would ever find them. Meanwhile, the doctor relaxed against a solitary palm tree, serene and still.

"Dr. Smith, how can you be so calm?" cried Reginald. "We're going to die on this God-forsaken island! No one will ever find us here!"

"Listen to me," commanded the doctor. "Five years ago, I gave the United Givers $500,000 and another $500,000 to the Consortium of Jewish Givers. I donated the same amounts again the following year. Three years ago, when I did very well in the stock market, I contributed $750,000 to each. Last year business was good again, so the two charities each got a million dollars."

"So what? How will that save us now?" protested Reginald.

"It's time for their annual fund drives," replied Dr. Smith with a smile. "They'll find me."

Many people of means pursue anonymity, not necessarily out of humility, but because they don't want to get hassled by a never-ending stream of fundraisers, charities and ministries seeking their financial support.

Fear and guilt tend to drive our focus inward as we try to protect ourselves from others' judgments, cutting remarks or persistent appeals. Consequently, for many years Susie and I tried to hide our wealth by living understated lives (see *Living with Wealth,* chapter 8, "Stealth Bomber"). I can tell you, it's not a satisfying way to live—and it's not necessary. Recognizing how fear and guilt can drive us is more than half the battle to overcoming both on the way to smarter generosity.

> Fear and guilt tend to drive our focus inward as we try to protect ourselves from others' judgments, cutting remark or persistent appeals.

Practical Issues

Beyond guilt and fear, a few very practical issues can hinder us from becoming the wisely generous people most of us feel called to be. For Susie and me, the three biggest practical issues were *lack of vision, artificial limits* on our giving, and *spousal disagreement.*

Lack of Vision

This challenge probably hinders more individuals from becoming generous than any other single factor. The Bible says, "where there is no vision, the people perish" (Proverbs 19:18, KJV). Believe me, without a vision, your giving dies, too.

Susie and I struggled early on with giving as generously as we wanted to, not because of an unwillingness or inability to give more, but because we lacked a clear understanding of our purpose and passion. We enjoyed giving to our *alma mater* and to our church, but our initial vision didn't encompass much more. We had a very small philanthropic world, compared to our capacity to give.

Twice in the last fifteen years, we have found ourselves with a much greater capacity to give than what our then-current vision could support. I am not sure what feels more frustrating, a great vision without the resources to accomplish it, or plentiful resources with no idea about how to use them. (I'll discuss this issue in more depth in the next chapter.)

Artificial limits

During our journey toward smarter philanthropy, we discovered to our surprise that we often put artificial limits on how much we gave. Two primary factors played a major role in our construction of these artificial limits: the tithe, and the size of the gift.

The Tithe. If you were to ask many Christians what a believer should give, they will respond, "ten percent, which is called a tithe." For an average household, a ten percent gift is a significant and sacrificial gift; but for the person of capacity, it is not necessarily so.

> Jesus is far more concerned about the spirit of the gift than he is the amount.

I often hear Christians speak of the 10 percent tithe as a kind of speed limit. Once you have given your ten percent, you are free to do whatever you please with the other 90 percent. But good biblical stewardship does not say that ten percent of what you have is God's and the rest is yours. It is *all* God's! We are just as responsible for the stewardship of what we keep as for what we give away.

Did you know that, in the Bible, while Jesus talks about money a great deal, he mentions the tithe only twice? Matthew 23:23 and Luke 11:42 report the same incident, and in the other occurrence, Jesus speaks of the tithe only to show how the Pharisees used it as a measuring stick to "prove" their righteousness (Luke 18:12).

Why would one's righteousness end at ten percent? God does not tell us, "Be ten percent holy, because I am holy." Jesus is *far* more concerned about the spirit of the gift than he is the amount. When you read his many stories about how he wants people to give, you see that he measures and celebrates generosity, faithfulness and willingness. He sees giving, in fact, as an act of worship.

The apostle Paul builds on the same thought in 2 Corinthians 9:7 when he writes, "Each of you should give what you have decided in your heart to give, not reluctantly or under compulsion, for God loves a cheerful giver." The longest sustained passage on giving anywhere in the Bible is found in 2 Corinthians 8-9, and the writer never once mentions the tithe. He does, however, talk quite a lot about "grace."

The Size of the Gift. In time, we discovered that we had placed an artificial limit on ourselves regarding the size of our gifts. For most people, a gift of $5,000 to $10,000 represents a significant amount of money. But the time came when our capacity to give, coupled with specific requests from ministry partners, reached the $25,000 level and above. We had great difficulty even thinking in those terms and found ourselves reluctant to respond. Our problem was not lack of funds; it just seemed like an awful lot of money to give to a single organization. We wrestled with a cluster of fears, from creating an unhealthy dependency to opening the floodgates for future requests. We had now become "major donors."

But a strange and wonderful change happened when we eventually made a grant of $25,000 to an organization. We felt, in that moment, as though we had broken through a "glass ceiling" and were totally freed from all artificial limits to our giving.

Our artificial limit was $25,000; yours probably lies somewhere else. Whatever that limit may be, don't let fear constrain your giving. Be cautious, yes! We can create harm with large gifts, and in many ways (see Chapter 8, *Do No Harm*). But God *always* leads by faith. Sometimes a faith answer is "no" rather than "yes."

Spousal Disagreement

At one point or another, most of us who are married have disagreed with our spouses over our philanthropic giving. Susie and I certainly did! I've already told you how we handled our conflict, but every couple must deal in their own way with their particular disagreements. Your conflict might concern how much to give, or when to give, or to whom or what to give, or how often to give, or whether to give anonymously or openly—there may be as many kinds of disagreements as there are couples.

> God *always* leads by faith. Sometimes a faith answer is "no" rather than "yes."

I'm no marriage counselor, but may I recommend that regardless of how you solve your disagreement, you do so in a way that honors both parties? If one "wins" and the other "loses," then you haven't really solved anything; you've only managed a cease-fire that will surely erupt into open warfare sooner or later. (**Probably sooner.**)?

Most of all, remember that we're talking about generosity here. So how can both of you be generous in your spirits with each other?

In Search of Passion

A visitor to Vienna attended a recital and concert at the Strauss Auditorium. He felt deeply impressed with the architecture and the acoustics. He asked the tour guide, "Is this amazing auditorium named after Johann Strauss, the famous composer?"

"No," answered the guide. "It is named after Fred Strauss, the writer."

"Never heard of him," replied the tourist. "What did he write?"

"His name on a check," explained the guide.

With all the grants we have made in the last fifteen years, only once did we give permission to have our name posted on a building, and in that case, we recognized some good and prudent reasons for doing so. The same may hold true for you. Normally we elect not to have naming rights on any edifice to which we contribute, but that reflects our temperament and convictions—no one else's.

Don't allow any of *my* personal preferences to constrain or limit *your* giving. Identify what obstacles have kept you thus far from becoming as generous as you'd like to be, and then take practical steps to overcome or eliminate those obstacles.

What do you feel passionate about?

What kind of mission will your giving allow you to serve?

How would you describe the vision that drives you in this time, at this stage of your life?

I'd like to investigate those questions next.

Chapter 5

Mission, Vision, and Values

It's not hard to make decisions when you know what your values are.
ROY DISNEY

I have lost count of the number of times people have asked me how we set up our family foundation. The great irony is that, most of the time, the question has come from successful business people who saw overseeing a foundation as totally unlike running a business.

Well, it is and it isn't.

The two are the same in that most of the necessary steps to establishing a successful business apply equally to an effective foundation. In both cases, one must start by clearly defining the organization's mission, vision and values.

But the two differ in that, whereas the individual probably has very clear, defined goals and values in the business world, he or she may have invested very little time in thinking about appropriate goals and values in the philanthropic world.

"Isn't giving just giving? How hard can it be? Why do I need a clear understanding of mission, vision and values to guide me in the way *I* give?" they may ask. "Who's going to turn down free money?"

I think the following account of an earnest but confused young man can help answer those questions.

Why Do You Need Them?

One evening, a young woman brought her fiancé home to meet her parents. The mother and father agreed that, after dinner, the dad would try to learn more about this young man through careful conversation. He invited the fiancé to his study for a talk.

"So, what are your plans?" the father asked.

"I want to be a biblical scholar," he replied.

"A biblical scholar, hmmm?" the father said. "Admirable! And what will you do to provide a nice house for my daughter?"

"I will study," the young man replied, "and God will provide for us."

"I see," said the father. "And how will you buy her a beautiful engagement ring, such as she deserves?"

"I will concentrate on my studies," the young man replied, "God will provide for us."

"And children?" asked the father. "How will you support children?"

"Don't worry, sir, God will provide," replied the fiancé.

The conversation proceeded like this, and each time the father questioned, the young idealist insisted that God would provide.

Later, the mother asked, "How did it go, honey?"

The father answered, "He has no job and no plans, and he thinks I'm God!"

That young man had a clear *vision*— "In the future, I see myself as a biblical scholar"—but no *mission* or *values* to match. Why did he want to become a biblical scholar? What did he hope to accomplish? How would he know that he was fulfilling his calling? Answers to those questions would indicate his *mission*. How would pursuing that mission play out in real life? How would it impact the way he lived and how he treated his wife and family? What kind of legacy would he leave to his family, friends and colleagues? Answers to those questions would suggest his *values*. Without a mission and values to guide and give feet to a vision, most of us probably are destined for failure, like this young man—and in the process, we will likely hurt our loved ones the most.

Without a mission, vision and values statement to guide you and give feet to your life of giving, you likely will wind up frustrated, confused and hurt. The first step, then, is to invest extended time developing your personal mission, vision and values. In that way, you can guide and energize a successful life of philanthropy.

> Without a mission and values to guide and give feet to a vision, most of us probably are destined for failure,

Mission: Passion and Purpose

What is your "why"? What issues matter most to you? How would you describe your purpose in giving? "It is only through a sense of purpose," said Bill George, the former chairman and CEO of Medtronic, "that companies can realize their potential."[4] The same truth applies to foundations and charitable giving organizations.

Your mission provides your reason for being. It tells you what you're supposed to do. Typically, a mission changes very little over the course of many years, except for some refining. And where does such a mission come from? It comes from you, from your life experience and from what has captured your heart and soul.

What do you feel passionate about? What do you hope to accomplish through your giving? What kind of dreams would you like to see fulfilled? Do you want to make education affordable? Would you like to see a cure for multiple sclerosis? Do you long to help end racism? What makes your heart beat faster? The website for *US Trust* rightly states, "Philanthropy is most effective and sustainable when it is connected to what matters most to you."[5]

So . . . what matters most to you? Once you can identify *that*, you've moved a long way toward defining your mission.

> I believe you need to go with your calling, your heart, your passion. Asking which is most important would be like asking, "What's most important to you, your brain or your heart?"

I strongly caution you against trying to "choose what's more important." Deaf kids here or blind kids there? The starving in Africa or old folks in Los Angeles? The homeless nearby or the destitute far away? They're not equivalent or even comparable. This is why I believe you need to go with your calling, your heart, your passion. Asking which is most important would be like asking, "What's most important to you, your brain or your heart?" The heart needs the brain because the brain tells the heart to pump. And the brain needs the heart because the heart feeds it the blood it requires. They're interdependent; one is not "more important" than the other.

As a wise investor, you want to develop a taste for the needs that you understand best and in which you can invest most wisely. As a funder, you must make choices, not based on what others say is most important, but on what *you* feel called and equipped to do.

What interests you?

Almost certainly you should invest in areas where your passion, skills, background and story intersect in some way with a real need. Why? You'll probably be far more effective in an area where you have an enduring interest and history.

Vision: Focus and Method

Vision is your *what*. How do you plan to fulfill your mission, given your particular circumstances? As you survey the landscape and observe current trends, attitudes, demographics and other constantly-shifting factors, how do you think you can have an impact on changing the world, as you have dreamed? As you gaze into the future, what looks different *then* because of what you will do *now?*

"Mission and vision work together to define who you are, what you do, how you do it, for whom you do it, and where you want to go in the future," writes Don Jernigan, former CEO and president of Adventist Health System. "Mission and vision differ from one another, but they absolutely must join forces. If mission is the bow that provides the energy to send an arrow hurtling through the air, then vision is the string that transfers that energy to the arrow. The bow and the string have different functions, but if they don't work together, then the arrow misses the target."[6]

Unlike mission, which usually changes little over time, vision adapts itself to shifting realities. Let's say part of your mission is to tackle homelessness and improve high school graduation rates (you had to drop out of high school when your own family lost its home). Let's also assume that you now live in Chicago, Illinois, and you want to direct much of your giving to your community. But then you move to Snohomish, Washington. While your mission remains as important to you as ever, will the vision you employ in Snohomish look the same as it did in Chicago? Probably not. Changes in environment, demographics and other key factors usually require a change in vision, though not necessarily in mission.

Although I say "vision can change," you need a long-term perspective to your philanthropy. Don't mimic what some organizations, churches and philanthropists do, going into an area for three years merely to get photo ops and then quit. What successful business executive or investor says, "I'm going to do this for three years, and then I'll quit"? No, effective philanthropy needs a long-term perspective. If your vision radically changes every time you meet an acute need, then you probably need to revisit both your mission and your vision.

Values: Core and Soul

You could think of values as the behavioral norms of your organization. They describe how you "do business." Integrity, compassion, efficiency, loyalty, innovation—these kinds of qualities often get tabbed by many organizations as their core values.

What values do you want to characterize *your* giving efforts?

"If you think of vision and mission as an organization's head and heart," said Buzzotta, Lefton, Cheney and Beatty in *Making Common Sense Common Practice,* "[7] then the values it holds are its soul." Your values can, in fact, become more important than your mission and vision on a day-to-day level, because those values guide your daily decision-making. You may say, "We want people to be treated with compassion," or "We value humility and wholeness." Such values become the guardrails that keep you on track and out of the ditch. Values are "make-or-break" types of decisions.

If you are choosing a board of advisors, make sure that the prospective members share your values. While some leaders want board members who will do whatever they are asked to do, you need some critical thinkers on your board. You don't however, want someone who brings an agenda of his or her own, who attempts to hijack whatever you set out to do.

The Same But Different

While I have insisted that your mission will probably change little over time, and your vision may change now and then primarily because of new realities around you, recognize that your calling and passion may get refined over time. While they will not likely change massively, they will undergo some sharpening.

At one time, Sacred Harvest funded only one international ministry; all other funding went to domestic organizations. But then I heard the late Dr. John Stott, an Anglican priest, say that our passions should never negate God's passions—and God has a passion for the world. I concluded that we absolutely had to address this issue. Today, about a third of our grant money goes to international concerns . . . but it took us five years to get there.

A whole universe of need is out there, with all kinds of demands: core issues, emergent issues, catastrophes, long-term problems. While you may understand a certain area and feel passionate about it, perhaps another concern cries out for your attention, though you don't yet even know it. A dance plays out between your understanding of your own skills, background, history, passion, and that universe of diverse needs.

I recommend that you select a specific concern for your initial focus, and then find organizations that do effective work in that space. This becomes a feedback loop as you learn from these organizations and you begin to say, "I *really* care about this."

It Takes Time

Wise corporate executives don't put business plans in cement, because they know those plans must remain adaptable and flexible. No one can fully foresee the opportunities and obstacles that lie before them.

Every boxer will tell you that no fight strategy survives the first punch. And every general will tell you that no plan of attack survives the first shot. So, who wins? Usually the one who can adapt the fastest.

In a *Harvard Business Review* article titled "Discovery-Driven Planning,"[8] McGrath and MacMillan insisted that new ventures require a new way of planning. Instead of a business plan built around

> The most robust enterprises adapt their assumptions and remain flexible with their strategies.

immutable assumptions that never merit any questioning or testing, you must create a process to systematically uncover, test, and (if necessary) revise the assumptions behind your venture's plan. Why? Because every new venture encounters unanticipated headwinds or unforeseen opportunities. The most robust enterprises adapt their assumptions and remain flexible with their strategies.

This principle extends to the world of philanthropy. You begin with a broad net, having a general sense of where you want to go; but then you invest *a lot* of time and effort probing and exploring. Give yourself plenty of time for learning and discovery! Don't worry much about mistakes you may make along the way, but do learn from them. They are highly valuable.

A young man once approached his successful boss and asked, "What is the secret of your success?"

"I make right decisions," the boss replied.

"Well, how do I learn to make right decisions?" wondered the young man.

"You make right decisions based on experience," replied his mentor.

"And how do I get experience?" asked the frustrated young man.

"By making wrong decisions," his boss answered!.

Most philanthropic leaders need four to five years (there's that rule again) of probing, exploring and testing to begin to find the clarity and focus they need to define about 80-90 percent of what they want to do and be. Reflecting on these essential years will reveal much about yourself and your family.

Some individuals may not admit to having a defined process for how they give; their giving decisions look merely like intuition, a gut reaction. We operated that way for many years. But when my board finally got my attention and began to draw out of my wife and me why we gave where we gave, we began to recognize some unifying themes. From those, we built our original mission/vision and values statements (see chapter 3). As we became more intentional in our giving—rather than merely reacting to a good presentation—our mission, vision and values grew much clearer.

Does that process sound overwhelming to you? It's really not. Think of yourself as rowing a boat. The best way to row in a straight line is not by looking over your shoulder toward your destination, but rather by looking at the wake of your boat. If the wake is straight, then you are moving in a straight line toward your goal.

We can learn an almost limitless amount of information about ourselves by looking at the "wake" we leave behind us with our lives and our giving. When we look back, we can see where we have been, which helps us explore several questions: Why were we there? What did we learn? What excited us? What discouraged us? Does some thread connect all these events? If so, what is it? Children? Hunger? Evangelism? Justice? International missions? Churches? You might find more than one focus, but almost certainly you will find yourself returning to your "core" time and again.

This process never stops. So long as you operate, you must continue to test your assumptions and question your strategies. About every three years, I reflect at length on where we have been and what has excited us, which helps us to crystalize what is truly core to our philanthropy. I stop my regular activities for a while to look back and ask, "Okay, what about this attracted us? Why did we go for that?" We continue to test our strategy, looking back at what we did and why we did it. Then, knowing what we know today, we ask, "what would we do differently? Did we operate consistently?" Sometimes we conclude, "That wasn't a good fit for us."

Ask yourself why you did that grant, what got you really excited. Your giving patterns will yield many clues about who you are. Sören Kierkegaard said it this way: "Though life is lived forward, it is best understood backwards."

Don't be afraid to make mistakes! Someone once asked Michelangelo, "How did you sculpt a perfect David?" The great artist replied, "I kept chipping away that which wasn't David." We learn by exploring, probing and testing to see what works or doesn't. Don't worry too much if it doesn't work. You will have done well by eliminating one more thing that "isn't you."

Always keep in mind that the document you write describing your mission, vision and values is a *working* document. Although you probably will not eliminate or add any core item, the further you go in your philanthropic journey, the clearer your focus will become. Yet you will always make new discoveries and gain new understanding, which means your strategies and assumptions will be both tested and verified or sharpened.

And all of that's good.

Goals or Directions?

A friend recently asked me about my "ten year strategy." Frankly, I have always struggled with establishing specific, strategic goals, such as, "By such-and-such a time, we will have achieved a certain number of X." This perceived weakness bothered me until a friend helped me to see that I appear to think and lead in "directions" instead of goals. As we set out in a direction and go forward patiently, we discover that many unanticipated opportunities present themselves that fit within our mission, vision and values. One staff member says I operate with "strategic directions looking for strategic opportunities."

> I have come to see that God often leads me where I never expected to go.

During our fifteen years at Sacred Harvest, I have come to see that God often leads me where I never expected to go. Yet when I get there, I find that what He has placed before me fits very well within our core purpose. I did not run away in search of a "shiny new object." I've found it helpful to meditate on a thought-provoking truism: "In their hearts humans plan their course, but the Lord establishes their steps" (Proverbs 16:9, NIV).

In the book of Acts, God often led Jesus' disciples in directions they never intended to go. But "stuff happens," in their lives and in ours (see chapter 18, "Stuff Happens," in *Living with Wealth Without Losing Your Soul*). The disciples faithfully took the next step of faith, never knowing exactly what might transpire. The next step is often all that God gives us. We must remember that "God is a lamp unto our feet," not a searchlight into our future.

And yet, *everywhere*, at *all* times, "God is light" (1 John 1:5).

Since I have not written a book of theology here, I have no desire to tease out the many amazing ways in which God brings life-giving light and guidance into our lives. On the other hand, I believe I would shortchange you if I didn't declare my deep conviction that God Himself constantly works in us--often in unnoticed ways—to inspire and guide the mission and vision that ends up directing our philanthropic efforts.

No doubt our own passion and experience work together to inform most of that direction, but I would insist that the God "who dwells in unapproachable light" (1 Timothy 6:16) ultimately lies behind every good impulse that drives us.

For me, that's far more than a heartwarming sentiment or a quaint religious opinion. It gives me hope when I feel lost, strength when I feel weak, and confidence when doubt rattles me. I love the way the prophet Isaiah put it: "Let him who walks in darkness and has no light trust in the name of the Lord and rely on his God" (Isaiah 50:10). When your own path seems murky, do you ever feel as though you walk in darkness? My path often looks unclear to me--but that's when I especially need to trust in the Lord, because although I can't see beyond the next step, He can.

Best of all, perhaps, I can testify that even when I stub my toe in the dark, God delights in taking that painful misstep and turning it into something wonderful. I often say that God is the world's greatest recycler: He uses even our junk and transforms it into the kind of treasure that glorifies Him and serves others.

All Foundations Are Unique

I like the adage that says, "If you have seen one foundation, you have seen one foundation." Every foundation is unique in its purpose and scope.

Just as each individual shares similarities with other individuals, but no two humans are exactly alike, so also do all foundations share certain similarities, although each one has a unique mission, vision and core values. A tremendous amount of diversity exists in how, where and when foundations give resources—and that's nothing but wonderful.

If you find yourself in our former situation of excess resources and no clear vision, let me encourage you. When you truly desire to learn how you would like to invest, be patient; eventually it will be revealed to you, either within your current giving profile or through another unforeseen opportunity.

And you can take that to the bank—so to speak.

Chapter 6

Leadership is Everything

People buy into the leader before they buy into the vision.
JOHN MAXWELL

I once spoke with an investment banker, a member of my church, in hopes of better understanding how he vets a company for his business. "We always begin by studying the leadership of the company," he said, "beginning with the CEO and the board. Leadership is everything to us."

People give to people, it is often said, and I believe that's mostly true. The same principle holds true for investing: people invest in people. Without question, at Sacred Harvest we look for leaders of organizations that we think can make a difference in their corner of the world, especially if someone can give them a little help.

What do we look for in such leaders?

We Look for a Good Idea

We search primarily for leaders of charitable organizations that have a clearly defined mission and strategy. We want to help the leaders take that great idea, develop it, achieve sustainability, and maximize their impact.

We are not angel investors; we don't accept start-ups. Call us "venture philanthropists," if you will. From our perspective, a ministry seeking our help must already have identified the significant need it seeks to address, and then have a great vision for how to meet that need. Leaders must have developed these ideas already and must be committed to them. Our foundation's role, then, is to help provide the capacity to make that idea work in the real world.

As a grantor, your primary role is to provide the capacity to help these leaders achieve their goal. At the same time, don't feel surprised when you find yourself working with your ministry partner to craft or hone the idea.

Any organization that seeks funding from Sacred Harvest must have leaders with a clear understanding of who they are and what they are trying to do. A leader who doesn't know these things has not developed clarity about his or her mission, and therefore tends toward "mission drift." And we don't fund mission drift.

_____

We invest in capable
leaders, not dreamers.

_____

We seek leaders with a great idea, but even more importantly, we need to find leaders who have the ability and a clear strategy to deliver. Many leaders around the world call themselves visionaries, and nearly everyone loves a clear and definable vision. But too often these self-described visionaries are little more than dreamers. They can produce seven new ideas every day but lack the ability to develop a road map to achieve any of those dreams. We invest in capable *leaders,* not dreamers.

The men and women we seek do not need to be "A+" leaders, but the leaders we ultimately select will demonstrate a willingness and desire to become better and more competent at leading. We want a leader who is willing to grow and who is willing for us to grow along with him or her.

We do not insist that every leader we fund must have the qualities required to run a Fortune 500 company; in fact, to require such a skill would be harmful. Many excellent non-profits serve the greater good of their community in an impactful way because their leaders have a heart and passion for their work. Yet some of these leaders do not possess, and possibly could not develop, the traits necessary to grow their non-profit to a larger scale.

We work with several organizations in which the leaders seem ideally suited to serve their small constituency. They have neither college degrees nor a tremendous business sense; they simply love and care for their people to the greatest extent their talents allow. To judge them for not desiring to grow a larger organization, or to press them to become more sophisticated than they are, is to do them a grave disservice. And it could quite possibly harm the mission.

Many leaders serve small communities precisely because they are wired that way. To require them to run their non-profit like a well-oiled business demands a skill set they simply do not have or even desire. They do not have to be organized like a major charity for us to decide to partner with them, but by law, certain basic accounting, funding and governance standards must be met. And that is why we fund so many training initiatives.

A word of caution that we learned the hard way: every leader must be evaluated *regarding the size and scope of his or her mission, not someone else's*. It is wrong to make false comparisons (compari-sins?) ? by judging one leader or organization against another.

Training: An Excellent Lever

We love to step in with training opportunities to help bring growing leaders up to speed. We consider this a great investment with the potential to have a tremendous impact, not necessarily to expand the ministry, but to help it become sustainable and maintain its effectiveness.

Many non-profit leaders, especially those who lead small organizations, *manage* better than they *lead*. They landed in this role because they feel passionate about the work; but the next thing they know, they have staff, a board and donors. These leaders generally have a lower level of capability and a lesser understanding of the business side of running an organization, though they still manage to meet a critical community need.

In 2013, therefore, we began to sponsor the Mission Increase Foundation office in Orange County. We did so out of our desire to provide necessary training for non-profit leaders to enhance their skills in fund development. By offering this training opportunity, we can help leaders develop a greater capacity to fundraise, for example. We may be wiser to invest $10,000 in a matching grant that helps leaders develop a critical fundraising skill than to spend $20,000 elsewhere. In this way, our ten grand can greatly multiply.

We developed an additional training program in 2015, The Organizational Health Pathway, to help build the competencies and capabilities of the leader and the organization. This training focuses on addressing three fundamental needs of all non-profits (although they always tend to think that more money solves everything):

➤ Governance
➤ Strategic planning
➤ Operational planning

These three needs, once met, will enhance effectiveness, efficiencies and impact.

Key Characteristics of a Fundable Leader

At Sacred Harvest, we use a measurement tool that helps us evaluate which leaders appear to have a good possibility of working successfully with us on a project. We look for eight specific traits to see if there might be a good match between these leaders and us.

1. Teachability

Are they able to listen to and learn from others? Do they seek to grow as leaders and so improve their organizations? A good leader (grantors, too) must be willing to receive input.

2. Accountability

Do they have a board to whom they are accountable? A friend of mine who has been making grants for three decades always asks the leader, "Who can fire you?" If the leader has no answer, my friend doesn't grant to the organization.

3. Affability

Do they "play well with others?" Do they cooperate with other organizations to coordinate activities and services in order to avoid duplication? Do they have effective partnerships that help leverage their ability to serve, or do they seem interested only in making a name for themselves?

4. Transparency

No organization is without challenges, whether financial, staffing, strategy, tactics, or a million other concerns. Many leaders eagerly tout their strengths and accomplishments, and rightly so—but do they also see their weaknesses and perceive their threats? Are they willing to admit them openly and honestly? When a charity willingly speaks of its challenges, we have great confidence in the leadership. Why? Because these leaders already know what they need to address.

5. Integrity

Are they trustworthy? If you give them a restricted gift, will they do what they say they will with it, or will they use those resources for something else without seeking the grantor's permission? You might be surprised to learn how often this "bait and switch" practice takes place among non-profits.

6. Self-awareness

If leaders in the organization have no self-awareness, if it's all rosy and good, then somebody's living on an Egyptian river called "Denial." If leaders don't recognize and own their problems or their weaknesses, we don't want to touch them. For us, bad news ("we haven't done this well") is often good news: it reveals to us that the leaders understand the obstacles before them.

7. Long-term perspective
Do the leaders have an enduring, long-term perspective regarding their work? They are not just running in and running out. They are in for the long haul.

8. A love for their people
Do the leaders have an endearing love for those they serve, empowered by a passionate commitment to their cause? To the best of their ability, do they lovingly tackle whatever they have felt called to do?

Whenever we see this cluster of eight traits in a leader, our interest grows. This leader may not yet be an "A player," but we want to see if she or he might have the capacity to grow and lead more effectively.

Humility, The *Sine Qua Non*
The wisest people I know, and probably the most successful, are those who willingly acknowledge that they don't know what they don't know. Humility is a critical ingredient for all learning; without it, learning stops.

All of us can always find something to learn or unlearn, even in our own areas of so-called expertise. Philanthropy is no different. Therefore, *the overarching quality we look for in a leader is humility.*

All of us, ministry leaders and grantors alike, must begin with a deep sense of humility. It simply doesn't work, otherwise. It can't. If you are venturing into a charitable giving enterprise for the first time, then you really have no option but to step into the journey with humility. The way down is the way up. Saint Augustine once said, "Do you wish to rise? Begin by descending. You plan a tower that will pierce the clouds? Lay first the foundation of humility."

Leaders We Avoid

Many energetic leaders of small organizations dream up three grand schemes and five breathtaking new projects every year, and we think, *But you can barely raise enough money for one!* They just throw them out there, hoping that at least one might excite a funder.

Many other leaders just can't delegate. They can paint a beautiful picture of some exciting initiative, but then they insist on controlling every detail. They refuse to hand off responsibility and build other leaders under their influence. We often view this as a fundamental flaw, when the leader's identity becomes so confused with the non-profit that everything revolves around her. The best leaders are team players. They know how to elicit the best from their people and how to motivate and involve their constituents. They live by the motto, "There is no measure of what can be achieved when you don't care who gets the credit."

> They live by the motto, "There is no measure of what can be achieved when you don't care who gets the credit."

If you're thinking about starting a foundation, or if you have just begun one, you should know about these sticky issues. You will deal with exactly these kinds of leaders. You must interact with men and women who have great vision, right up to their level of incompetence (the Peter Principle).[9] These leaders just don't want to let go. The size or scope of their organization exceeds their capability--so you simply can't give them money.

Get to Know the Leader

I doubt you can really know the leaders of potential ministry partners without meeting them as close to *their* space as you can get. How can you understand any of what you really need to know from only what you can read? I am convinced that a relational site visit connection is crucial.

The most effective plan is to meet with leaders in the field and ask them, "What is the real need out here? What are you passionate about? What is the core challenge for your organization?" Seek to learn what a leader wouldn't normally tell you. "What do you typically not tell funders? I want to hear the truth about what's really going on."

I love the times when we can go out and meet ministry leaders just to invest time in listening, without an agenda, and hear their needs and challenges. But I love even more when we can clearly see (or create) an alignment between our goals and purposes and theirs.

Do you *really* want to know? If so, then visit them *in their space*. And then listen.

Chapter 7

Be Relational

If you want to go fast, go alone. If you want to go far, go together.
AFRICAN PROVERB

One of the biggest concerns we encounter in our interactions with non-profit leaders, whether faith-based or not, is the deep sense of isolation they feel. Clearly, they have a lot of human contact throughout the day, but the majority of that contact is based on work and performance. When board members or staff personnel speak with them about an issue, often that communication revolves around achieving goals, fixing problems or solving conflicts. But to whom can they turn when they begin to struggle personally with various difficulties? They typically find it very tricky to confide in either their staff or board members.

The same can be said about donors. As grant makers, we can very easily feel dehumanized, as though needy people constantly want to make us into ATM machines. We can quickly lose our understanding that we are dealing with real human beings, called to serve the needs of others. Especially on bad days (and we all have them), the grantor can treat the grantee like a supplicant, a beggar, a dirty little serf with his hands held out and his palms up.

I know. I have been there.

I admit that donors can find it difficult to have meaningful relationships with leaders of every organization they support, especially if they grant to forty-plus ministries (as we do). Sometimes we give a grant to an organization simply because we value its work, even though we have no intention of building a partnership with that organization or its people. Still, we try our best, with the tremendous aid of our staff, to be consistently relational with those whom we consider to be our core partners. We do this, in part, by providing regular professional support and encouragement to our grantees.

More than a Transaction

We desire a genuine partnership with the people and organizations we help to fund. That's our goal.

Whenever possible, we want to make every grant not merely a transaction, but a conduit for developing a real relationship. We desire a genuine partnership with the people and organizations we help to fund. That's our goal.

We partner with one organization that works with children trying to survive terrible home and living situations. Many of these children suffer from PTSD-like symptoms. Perhaps a little boy saw his mother's boyfriend forcibly hold her down on the floor, beat her and tear out chunks of her hair. Maybe other children saw a friend, cousin or brother shot to death right in front of them, or they grew up in a crack den. Unless you can somehow begin to address the spiritual and emotional needs of these children, come to understand something of their plight and try to walk with them through this psychological and spiritual darkness, then you had better not get into the game. Without an understanding of their situation—which can come only through relationship—you can't do much good in arenas like this, and you can instead do actual harm. If you start touching things you don't even know, you can create more problems than solutions.

Just getting these adolescents a job through a nice grant won't cut it. You must see that they get care for their whole being, which involves walking with them on difficult pathways. As donors, we cannot personally help all the kids we want to help through these dark situations, but we can walk with the people who provide the services we fund. We can get some understanding of the true situation through these providers, but we won't gain that necessary understanding unless we commit to a genuine relationship.

One of our board members recently told me about a trip he took to India to visit a group of twelve women from a remote village. They had received funding to sell products designed to help them become self-sufficient. He and others in his group interviewed these women as part of an initial impact survey. All the women said their little group provided them with tremendous assistance, and not just economically. They told of feeling deeply encouraged because they are a part of this little peer group. The economic empowerment funded by a small grant flowed down to all sorts of other areas of life. They could now pay for their children to go to school. Their in-laws didn't beat them anymore. They are learning how to be more relational.

The first level of these success stories is *always* relational. The deeper matters and soul issues of life always flow out of human-to-human contact. That's the gospel. Transformation occurs through relationships, and that is where we believe we must start. If we don't start there, we run the very real risk of not addressing the real issues.

Transformation simply doesn't happen without a life-for-life exchange. But what does that mean for us, if we cannot develop close relationships with all the people affected by the grants we provide? What does it mean, if we can't even draw near to all the leaders of the organizations we help fund? We have no choice but to walk with as many ministry leaders as possible in the places where they serve. To the degree we manage that tightrope walk, we become more knowledgeable, effective, and successful in our own philanthropic work.

The Advantages of Relationship

We see many significant advantages in building genuine relationships with leaders of our partner organizations. When we nurture a trusted relationship with organizational leaders, we not only come to know the strengths and weaknesses of the organization, we also gain the credibility to speak into the life and needs of the organization. Doing this helps us to become more strategic in our granting.

Sometimes being a good grantor means being a good friend (and occasionally like being a good parent). With that kind of relationship, you can help the organization's leaders navigate a course that helps them become stronger and healthier, whether as individuals or as an organization.

One of the leading foundations in Orange County often receives feedback from the community leaders it serves about the value of the relationships these leaders have with representatives of the foundation. Many of these leaders say, "We value these relationships more than the grants we have received." All leaders crave relationships they can trust, relationships that make it clear the grantors are committed to their success and well-being, both personally and organizationally. As donors, we get to play that role. We consider it a sacred trust, a calling.

At the same time, these leaders need more than donor friends and supporters. Effective grant-making sometimes requires every part of us—our gifts, abilities, wisdom, experience, and yes, our resources. Leaders and organizations need relationships that can offer them varied resources and skill sets.

Perhaps one grantor approaches grant-making from an analytical level, looking carefully at the numbers, while another looks at the same issues from a more philosophical perspective. This kind of dynamic interplay happens best in the context of relationship. Decisions made in that context result in better decisions—which is important, frankly, because the grant-making world often can become a really bizarre place.

Citizens of a Common Realm

If you haven't lived in the trenches before you stepped into this wonderful-but-sometimes-odd grant-making space, you can unknowingly make a somewhat weird environment even more weird. It's very easy, for example, to treat the organizations coming to you for support as if they were peasants coming to the king, pleading for their daily bread.

Equally, organizations can feel intimidated by your power and position. The wisest approach comes not from a place of power or position, which can feel very threatening, but from viewing grantees as peers. Our Filipino program officer has often told us about potential grantees feeling nervous before an interview, even to the point of tears, because they have never talked to Americans. As donors, we depend as much on the grantee for the success of our investment as they depend on us for the funds to make the project a reality. You'll often hear a fun description of our work around our office and from our board members: "We grow our fruit on other organizations' trees."

"How might we do that?" you ask.

Find advisers who can help you to effectively do what you want to do. Bring in the talents and skills you don't have. You might be great at business or fantastic with technology, but you may never have needed to think through the hard side of business or the difficulties of leading a non-profit. Bring together a board filled with wise, skilled individuals, and get advisers who can give you an accurate picture of the non-profit world. Second, if you can, hire staff members or consultants who can provide this relational face for you.

Above all, always—*always*—remember that the primary level is relational. It really is all about relationship. We're all citizens of the same realm.

None of Us Can Survive Alone

All of us came into this world as relational beings. While some of us do better at relationships than others, none of us can survive alone. I have never been able to forget a news story I heard decades ago that cemented this conviction in my soul.

At the beginning of the twentieth century, orphanages in the United States began reporting a higher than normal rate of infant mortality for the children in their care. What caused this tragic situation--and more importantly, what could cure it? Investigators eventually identified the culprit as a lack of human contact. The babies had been left alone in their beds for long periods of time without any human touch. As workers began to hold the babies and interact with them every day, the mortality rate for these infants quickly returned to normal.

All of us need regular human contact. We all require real relationships, person-to-person connections. Health comes with daily human interaction—and as donors, we can build relationships with leaders in our partner organizations that can work wonders for everyone involved.

Chapter 8

Do No Harm

First, do no harm.

HIPPOCRATES

All physicians take the Hippocratic oath to "do no harm." As doctors endeavor to get their patients healthy, they take great care to ensure that their efforts do not make the sick even sicker.

Grantors must be equally aware that the funds they make available can unintentionally hurt or even destroy organizations, or divert them from their missions. Remember the basic rule: "Good intentions are never enough." We must be wise to avoid causing damage with our grant dollars, which leads to my first instruction to those just getting started in philanthropy:

"First, do no harm."

I sometimes get strange looks when I make this statement. I can almost see the mental gears turning: *How could giving away money harm anyone? That's so easy!* And on one level, it is. Who refuses free money? What could be easier than handing out dollars?

But it worries me when men and women come into great sums of money and suddenly want to be philanthropists. They have little background in philanthropy. They're just wealthy Americans with a deep desire to address the problems of their world. They want to make a positive difference.

But giving *wisely* turns out to be the hardest part of all.

A Holistic Approach

Doing work in this space without doing harm requires a tremendous amount of effort. Maybe you observe a poverty situation and say, "We want to solve that terrible problem." But then you find it's intricately linked to countless other issues, all interwoven: corruption, drugs, violence, limited access to credit, poor education, few opportunities, broken homes, caste systems, poor health, welfare dependency. Thinking that you have found the solution, you pull on one thread—and watch the whole thing unravel.

The most effective organizations take a holistic approach, which comes only through patient learning. We must move forward slowly when we initiate change in the world of philanthropy.

In the Third World, building relationships comes before providing answers. We Americans tend to have a lot of hubris: after all, we are "First World" and college-trained! We know best! So, forget culture. Ignore anyone else's God-given abilities and capabilities. Just jump in and try to orchestrate everything from the beginning, rather than building slowly, adapting to the culture and the people's natural abilities and resources.

We recently spoke with leaders of a megachurch in Singapore who wanted to send hundreds of their members to the Philippines on short-term mission trips, many times a year. The church wanted its people to experience Filipino life.

Hundreds invading at one time? The idea horrified us.

"The leaders must go and build relationships and learn," we said. "They can't just bring an army of people. There are grave dangers in doing for others what they can do for themselves. The potential harm is enormous if they don't do this wisely." This church has 5,000 members and wants to find multiple places around the world where it can send its members for short-term "experiences." The great danger of such an altruistic endeavor lies in assuming that we know what the local people need better than they do, and that we can do it better than they can.

Three books have helped Sacred Harvest avoid the mistakes typical of many well-intentioned donors. I highly recommend:

Toxic Charity, by Bob Lupton[10]
Serving With Eyes Wide Open, by David Livermore[11]
When Helping Hurts, by Brian Fikkert[12]

All three of these books will provide you with hard-earned wisdom that can help you succeed where success counts the most. (For other helpful resources, please see the Recommended Reading List in Appendix A.)

Money Can Hurt

On one of our first grants to an organization in the Philippines, we did a poor job of due diligence. We gave a capital grant to build a new training center and school, but about halfway through the project, the funded group ran out of money. A bad estimate of cost had doomed the project from the start. What an embarrassment!

Despite our good intentions, they weren't happy, and neither were we. We never realized until then how painful such a failure could be. We missed and they missed. We simply misunderstood their capacity; we assumed too much. On their end, they invested in a big project that they never would have undertaken except for us, and it hurt them.

They had to come back to us, asking for more money to complete a half-finished building. We took responsibility for what we had done to worsen the problem, and to correct the blunder, we hired a consultant to vet the cost of finishing the project. We have now added this step on all our building grants.

We have also created harm by funding a staff position for just one year, only to discover that the organization could not find the money to maintain the position for succeeding years. As a result, the position had to be eliminated.

Too often donors make a grant for a new staff position or to start a new program, without giving careful thought about where the organization will find the money to maintain the position or program. Sacred Harvest has decided that when we make such grants, we will fund them for three years, affording the organization the time to develop new resources to sustain the initiative. The first year, we usually provide full funding; in each of the second and third years, the grant amount gets reduced by one third.

Grantors also must realize that the dollars they invest into some projects can change a local economy, either for better or for worse. We once spoke with an organization working with tribal missionaries in the jungle. When an outside group came in and started paying the local men more than the norm, suddenly those extra dollars altered the whole economy. The outside group created a false financial system that created problems in that region.

Microfinance can cause similar problems. Some churches got into microfinancing with the idea that a basic loan would run eighty to one hundred dollars; their research said smaller loans could provide an economically sustainable model. And so a church might do microfinance for a few years, find it didn't work well for them, pull out of the programs and forgive the loan amounts. The result? Poor people learned that they didn't have to repay their loans. Such well-intentioned groups can poison the well by creating a model that trains recipients to "just wait for the next rich foreigners to arrive."

In his 2012 book, *Toxic Charity*, Robert Lupton writes of a delegation from an American church who visited a poor Latin American community to build a water well. Great idea, right? But the pump broke down within a year and remained broken until the church returned the next year to fix it. In a few months, it broke down again and stayed broken until the church came back once more to repair it. The church's giving created an unhealthy dependency that kept the local people from improving their lives. (Lupton released a second book four years later titled, *Charity Detox: What Charity Would Look Like if We Cared About Results*[13]).

I admit it: I also enjoy playing the role of the hero who saves the day. That's my greatest struggle, as it is for many others. I don't know if I have some hidden "messiah complex," or I just need to be the "fixer," or if it simply helps me feel good. Most of the time, it seems that just throwing a little money at the problem should solve it—and sometimes, such a strategy actually works. But in every case, despite how things may "look," we must strive to match our capacity to give with wisdom in giving.

> But in every case, despite how things may "look," we must strive to match our capacity to give with wisdom in giving.

Would anyone give a fifteen-year-old a no-limit MasterCard, without first taking the time to teach the young person how to manage those resources? Every good parent prepares a child to handle money. The same is true of a good grantor. We grant, always considering the long-term effect. Such thinking often results in constructing a grant specifically for the organization and its capacities, to make it more likely that those funds get managed effectively.

Finally, we must check our self-serving motivations at the door. Serving others merely to help us feel good about ourselves will lead to great harm. Of course, we *should* feel good about our granting! We *ought* to experience the joy of giving. But this good feeling must never happen to the detriment of those we want to help. When feeling good about ourselves becomes our primary motivation, bad things happen.

Relief Work Is Not Development

Relief work, whether responding to an earthquake in Haiti or to a tsunami in Indonesia, is an immediate and short-term response to an emergency. It usually involves providing food, water, shelter and medical care. The main purpose is to address a crisis with immediate aid.

Development, on the other hand, uses a long-term strategy to help people get back on their feet and become self-sustaining. Development helps people to re-establish themselves or raise their standard of living. Most poverty alleviation programs fall into this category.

Unhealthy dependence can easily occur if (1) relief work continues for too long, or (2) groups try to do development work with a relief mindset. The continent of Africa has suffered from large, charitable infrastructures that have existed for decades. To give relief for too long is to create unhealthy dependency. Likewise, if we confuse development work with relief work, we can create an unhealthy dependency on us and our assistance, rather than helping people to do what they can readily do for themselves.

We once tried to get a relief organization to add development work to its resumé. After three years of unsuccessful effort, we finally realized that while the group did tremendous relief work, long-term development simply was not in its DNA. So, instead of trying to change them, we decided to assist them as a primary provider of relief work in the Philippines.

Relief work requires a short-term strategy. It deals with critical needs at a specific time and place, plain and simple. Development requires a long-term strategy that attempts to change the whole landscape. It seeks growth.

Funding for the two activities differs significantly. Money rolls in after a front-page disaster, but when the catastrophe stops making the headlines, donations tend to dry up. Since we focus more on development, we don't live in that space. We do not address every natural disaster that occurs around the world. Our philosophy is that, if it appears on the front page, we don't participate . . . at least, not at first. We let the world respond. A year or two later, we may decide to get involved by supporting those doing redevelopment work.

A popular national park helps me to picture the difference between relief and development work. Have you ever visited Yellowstone? You'll see signs that say, "Do not feed the bears." Visitors think they are doing a good deed when they feed a hungry animal, but they unwittingly create an unsustainable ecosystem. Why? They don't stick around to keep feeding the animals. Their actions help them feel good, causing them to believe they're doing the right thing, but their lack of understanding the big picture causes them to end up doing more harm than good.

> Relief work requires a short-term strategy. It deals with critical needs at a specific time and place, plain and simple. Development requires a long-term strategy that attempts to change the whole landscape.

So, what can we do, as donors and philanthropists, to help the world rather than harm it?

A Few Suggestions

Sacred Harvest does not fund more than ten percent of an organization's yearly budget, and we prefer an even lower percent. With large organizations, that usually is not a problem. But the smaller organizations we tend to fund sometimes request operational grants that can easily exceed those guidelines.

In the Philippines, we typically do capital grants with small organizations that have yearly budgets of twenty, forty or a hundred thousand dollars. We prefer not to give them a forty-thousand-dollar grant. We've made exceptions, but not often. We tend to make such exceptions with organizations that have the capacity to deal with large capital gifts.

Fund raising is often a difficult and uncomfortable process for many non-profits; they feel tempted to repeatedly call upon the same set of willing donors. But what does this do to the long-term sustainability of the organization? It compromises it. What happens if those donors suddenly have a change of heart or quit, either due to donor fatigue from endless funding requests or simply because of death or loss of income?

Sometimes being a good donor means acting like a good parent. Just as you want your child to grow up to live independently without your ongoing financial support, so you need to help the organization grow up and become less dependent on you. We have found matching grants are a good vehicle for this, as they entice organizations to develop their own donor base.

> Sometimes being a good donor means acting like a good parent.

Our grants in the Philippines require each funded organization to have "skin in the game," often referred to as "counterpart." We never fund 100 percent of a project. Depending on the circumstances, the counterpart can include gifts in kind (e.g., construction materials, land), contributions of cash, volunteer labor or professional oversight.

We have been granting in the Philippines since 2005 and have purposely restricted how frequently a non-profit can propose a grant. We frequently say "no" to grant requests to force grantees to develop new donors within their own country.

Many development programs encounter problems in their efforts to change the condition of the poor through livelihood training or microfinance, if they neglect to address relevant character issues. We have found that the poverty cycle has as much to do with matters of character as it does with unjust financial systems or lack of resources.

Consider the many countries where men serve as the chief providers for their families. It is not uncommon to find these men spending their meager wages on wine, women and song. What do you think will occur when you help such men to increase their wages? Will more money flow toward their families? Not necessarily. They will then have even greater resources to spend on more wine, women and song, while their families continue to suffer. We have seen this story repeat itself over and over again.

As donors, we must always remember that money merely amplifies what is already in an individual's heart. More money in the hands of a fool only makes him a bigger fool.

On Getting Married

If you go too big, too long with funding an organization, you can find yourself "married." While you may not want to be married, you have lived with this group for so many years that they figure you're hitched through common-law. When the expected grant money suddenly disappears, therefore, the loss comes as a total shock to them.

To avoid this problem, at times we have funded operational support in a diminishing fashion, where each year the grant gets smaller, perhaps by one third each year. After the third year, the grant goes away.

Suppose we decide to make a lead gift on a capital campaign for one of our long-term partners. Even then, typically we don't want to be the sole provider. We want others to step in and induce additional groups to help. We always seek leverage, so we may create a challenge grant that gives the organization the leverage it needs to ask for other gifts.

All of us need to find ways of speaking into an organization to let it know that even though we may appear to be "married," the time may come when the union must dissolve. Such a reduction in or withdrawal of support could be triggered by a lack of confidence in the organization or its leadership, or merely because of a change of heart or direction in your granting.

Several years ago, we had a change of heart regarding our annual support of a ministry. I began asking, "How do we exit without doing great harm, knowing that our departure would create a significant hit to their budget?" We decided to make a gradual exit. We notified the group that we would reduce our support by half the next year, and after that, we would no longer support the ministry. We hoped this would give the group enough lead time to try to replace our funding.

Dissolving a "common law marriage" can get difficult when you operate with a relational approach to grant making. You must determine how to negotiate such sensitive interactions. Many foundations intentionally maintain distance precisely so they can remain objective. But in relational grant making, you must find a way to negotiate these tough issues.

In our opinion, the difficulty is worth the extra effort. Relationships are key to everything we do, and it is the relationships themselves—not just the work we do together—that prompt us to get out of bed each morning, eager to do it all over again.

Chapter 9

Practical Matters

*Take care, in reading the writings of philosophers or hearing
their speeches, that you do not attend to words more than things,
nor get attracted more by what is difficult and curious
than by what is serviceable and solid and useful.*

PLUTARCH

About three decades ago, author/illustrator David Macaulay created a whimsical and deeply informative book titled *The Way Things Work*. In a fun and fascinating way, he helped kids and adults alike understand how things worked, from parking meters to ultrasound. Perhaps best of all, he created a wooly mammoth to host his book, showing the beast hang gliding, roller skating, and in general having a fabulous time.

Just two years ago, Macaulay did a major update of his book—titled *The Way Things Work Now*—but this time using full color illustrations to give us practical insight into how current stuff really works, from WiFi to windmills.

While I'm no David Macaulay, in this chapter I'd like to suggest several practical matters for you to consider as you move along on your journey to smarter generosity. We've learned a few things in the last fifteen years about how philanthropy really works, so I want to focus on a few important practicalities of the work we do.

(Sorry, but no wooly mammoths. The closest I get is an MOU.)

Memorandum of Understanding

A Memorandum of Understanding (MOU) is an agreement, or covenant, agreed to by both grantor and grantee, in which each party promises to perform certain actions. You could just as easily call this a grant agreement.

We often use MOUs to manage expectations or to ensure accountability; an MOU works both ways. MOUs make it clear to our partners what they can expect from us, as well as what we expect from them. We don't make them super-complicated. This is critical, because we don't always remember accurately what was said in the conversation that led to the grant. As my favorite Chinese proverb says, "The faintest of ink is a thousand times more accurate than the sharpest memory."

Recently I sent our *alma mater,* Azusa Pacific University, the first check toward the expansion of a physical therapy facility. I soon received an email back from our contact, asking when to expect the next $500,000. I suggested he read the MOU.

"Steve," he replied, "I think we need to talk."

He sent me the memorandum, which clearly declared that we had agreed to send $1 million in that payment, not $500,000. Oops! I had acted on memory alone, and it bit me. They believed they were getting a million dollars, but they received a check for half that much. Now they had to approach the donor about it. If they didn't have that signed MOU, things could have gotten ugly.

We consider an MOU to be essential when a grantee enters a capital campaign. With an MOU in place, the organization can speak with confidence to other grantors/donors that certain monies have been pledged to its campaign, thus giving the potential donor confidence that the campaign has a measured chance of success.

For the grantor, the MOU ensures that the grantee will perform specific actions and honor the intent of the gift. All our MOUs require the grantees' board to fully approve the agreement, especially when we require the board to take some specific action. We do this because, at times, grantees receive funds for a specified project, only to 1) use those funds in a manner that the donor never intended, or 2) allow those funds to sit for many years until all the money gets raised, which in some instances may never happen. No grantor/donor ever wants to see a gift misused or appropriated for unintended projects, nor do they want their gifts to sit in a bank for years, waiting to be deployed.

A recent example of grant misappropriation made national headlines. An Ivy League university diverted some funds intended for an endowment to other projects. Because an MOU was in place, the granting family sued the university and won.

Fearful that a grant of ours for a science building could end up sitting in a bank for years until all the necessary funds got raised, Sacred Harvest requested in an MOU that the recipient and its board agree to be willing to borrow whatever funds might become necessary to complete the project. The agreement worked beautifully.

We utilize MOUs for other purposes than merely to preserve the intent and proper use of a grant. Not infrequently we determine that certain poor governance issues within a grantee organization must get addressed by the board before we will release a grant. Such an MOU specifies what the board must do or agree to do in order to receive the money.

In your communication with grantees, keep in mind the power imbalance that exists. They might not report unpleasant issues unless you make it open and safe for them to do so. Our MOUs make it easier for grantees to tell us when a grant isn't going well.

The MOU doesn't solve everything, of course; it is not some magic talisman that resolves all expectation problems. Before you even reach the MOU stage, therefore, you should get to know the grantee. That can take some time! You must travel down the road a bit with any possible ministry partner before even thinking of such an agreement. We don't grant to anyone we don't know; for us, an MOU is the *last* phase. Before that, it's all exploratory.

As stewards of the resources entrusted to us, we have a responsibility to see that any grants we make are used effectively and for their intended purposes. For that reason, the MOU has become one of our most potent tools.

The Benefits of Using Tranches

In most situations when we couple our grants with an MOU, the grant will get divided into tranches ("tranche" is a French word meaning "slice," "section," "series" or "portion"). We may divide the grant into as few as two segments or as many as necessary. Each portion of the grant gets released upon performance of certain agreed-upon action items.

We write a lot of grants in tranches. The idea is, "when you meet these goals, we release these funds." We do this even with operational funding. I do not necessarily trust an organization to manage a large lump sum for the whole year. Think of your favorite dog; you love him, but when you go on vacation, do you put out seven days' worth of food and leave? No. Why not? He'll eat it all in one day.

Sometimes in smaller, less sophisticated and less disciplined organizations, if you don't parse out a lump sum over the course of a year, they may say, "Ooh, look at all this money in the bank!" They might forget that it must stretch over 365 days. A tranche protects against that problem.

Support Operational Costs

I have served on enough boards to recognize one big threat that imperils the survival of many non-profits. It's not always a lack of funds, but that too many gifts are restricted and cannot be used to support day-to-day operations.

Once you get to know individuals in a non-profit on a deeper level, and they know that you want them to succeed, you'll often hear requests like this: "Please, give us general operating support." Many groups struggle mightily to obtain enough operating funds, while many grantors prefer to fund specific programs. The donors want all of their gifts to go to *this*. Meanwhile, the organization has fundamental operational needs, so it has to find other funds somewhere else to fill the gap.

We all enjoy the benefit of giving to a specific initiative. I have never met anyone who enjoys giving to a slush fund, where one has no idea how the funds will get used. A non-profit's difficulty arises when funds become so restricted that the organization lacks enough money to cover the cost of doing business: salaries, office expenses, utilities, or benefits.

Sacred Harvest tends to approach the problem as though the ministry *itself* were the program. If we trust the ministry's goals, aspirations and programmatic focus, then we *may* fund the operation so that it can continue to go out and do those good things. We anticipate that a lot of foundations will gladly join in to do the other projects.

If a certain non-profit has caught your attention and you want to enable its ongoing success, then consider funding at least part of its daily operations. At Sacred Harvest, we budget every year for the operational expenses of the ministries we consider to be our core partners; we give to their general fund. If they approach us with a specific grant request for a project or initiative, we might make an additional special grant for a restricted project.

Another way to accomplish the same end is to make a restricted gift that authorizes the ministry to use 10-20 percent of that gift to cover overhead costs. In capital campaigns, an enormous amount of staff time must be dedicated to the initiative's success, and the ministry somehow needs to recoup those expenses. Some non-profits build in a certain percentage of all campaign gifts to help cover the project's staff costs and expenses. This practice is most appropriate.

The concern of funding operations can become a tipping point. As a grantor, we can do harm by not funding enough or in the right categories. We can fail to take into account what it will actually cost to get the organization where it wants to go, or where we want it to go. We therefore must grant enough, and in the right spots, to enable the group to reach the tipping point for success. To fund an organization to the point where it *almost* gets there, but not quite enough to get over the hump, can cause harm. We can create the expectation of growth and excitement, without counting the cost of how much it will take to actually finish the job.

Get Proactive

Get proactive as you pursue opportunities within a current grantee list. If you trust and value a certain organization, you might consider meeting with the executive director or president to talk about strategic possibilities for further investment.

Other proactive methods require that you get more imaginative and creative. Think of ways in which you can use a grant to leverage the capability or capacity of an organization. Such an effort requires more intimate knowledge of the organization, but the more relational you are, the more effectively you can identify the often small but necessary leverage points that will either bring greater efficiency or effectiveness.

As a foundation, we enjoy working with smaller organizations, in part because our dollars have much more leverage and impact than giving to a mega-size organization. Also, these smaller groups are usually run by people who feel called to serve in a very focused way. They came together for a specific cause, with a passion to serve. As a former pastor, I often feel a need to bring encouragement and counsel that may help smaller groups flourish in their calling.

Regardless of size, all organizations need to cultivate new donors. A grantor can help with donor development, both old and new donors, in many innovative ways. Consider these three:

1. *Be willing to sponsor or host an event to raise funds.* This effort will not only help to bring greater awareness to the organization, but it will also serve to create a greater sense of community and partnership among donors.
2. *Offer a matching grant* to help the organization attract new friends, or to deepen the involvement of current friends.
3. *Sponsor a donor/staff appreciation event.* Such an event provides good leverage by helping to retain both donors and staff, two groups often taken for granted. Events like these make both donors and staff feel appreciated instead of "used." The loss of donors and staff often can become a big limiting factor to a ministry's continued success.

For reasons like these, I advise against zeroing out your charitable reserves each year in order to balance resources with vision. Maintaining a reserve affords you the opportunity to respond to unforeseen events and needs.

Learn How to Say "No"

Not all organizations are worthy of your "yes." When you need to say "no," which sounds better: "I don't want to give to your organization," or "I am sorry, but your organization does not fit our giving guidelines"?

Creating a defined mission, vision and value statement (see chapter 5), even a tentative one, can assist greatly in helping you determine to what causes and organizations you will give and not give. You need this, if for no other reason than it will prevent you from feeling guilty when you say "no" to some urgent request.

You probably need to steel yourself for those donors who will say, "How could you *not* give us money for [insert their project]? Everyone needs this!" Prepare yourself to say "no" to a hundred causes, all of them good. You must learn to say, "We have chosen to focus on these particular areas. We know a million nonprofits who are doing great work, but we cannot fund them all. We can go only with what's in our hearts. We must follow our passion, our calling."

And don't apologize!

Some of my friends who have journeyed much longer than me in this arena of philanthropy have suggested creating a nice "no" letter and then to practice saying "no" in a kind but clear way. You might choose to say, "Unfortunately, out of the twenty worthwhile projects we could support, our funds are already committed." Saying "no" gracefully is a real art, and a necessary one.

> Saying "no" gracefully is a real art, and a necessary one.

No doubt you will encounter outliers, grantees that you decide to fund outside of your core purpose. When you choose to make an outlier grant, you know that you do so because you believe in the group's mission, even though it does not perfectly align with yours. Sometimes, you just want to give a "love gift of support" to a worthy organization. Feel glad that you can!

Take Risks (and every grant is a risk)

Every grant we make is a step of faith. We place faith in both the leadership and in the organization to invest our money wisely. To minimize the risk, many donors choose to invest only in larger or historic organizations. Donors can do less monitoring with such a grant, because such organizations are more seasoned and experienced in grant management.

In general, the smaller or younger the organization, the riskier the granting. Sacred Harvest likes to leverage smaller organizations. We understand the risks and know that such a strategy requires more donor oversight to ensure that the organization stays true to its mission, to the intent of any restricted grants, and to maintaining sound fiscal management.

Regardless of the size or history of an organization, however, always assume you are taking some risk. Many donors have felt severely disappointed to see that an organization they supported for years has suddenly chosen to move in a different direction or is forced to close its doors. Instead of beating yourself up over such a loss or for failing to see it coming, be thankful for what you achieved during the time you helped fund the group.

And then move on.

There is a reason we refer to grant making as an "investment." Just as with the stock market, everyone hopes for a good or stable "return on investment" (ROI). Philanthropy is much like investing in the stock market or in some profit-making business; it is "informed risk." None of us should ever invest blindly. *If we let the risk of failure deter us from investing, we will never really invest.*

As you consider whether to invest in an organization, get the best information you can about both the organization and its leadership. Talk with other donors. Do your due diligence. Then, once you have achieved a level of confidence that feels comfortable to you, take the "leap of faith."

Chapter 10

Family Matters

If we fail, never give up because F.A.I.L. means "First Attempt In Learning."

APJ ABDUL KALAM

From day one, an important goal built into our family foundation was to use it as a platform to mentor our children in a life of philanthropy.

Though our children currently have no vote in the foundation, they do have a voice and are able to participate in our vision/mission trips with the organizations that Sacred Harvest supports. They also have met with and interviewed grantees, and from time to time, they even recommend granting opportunities that align with our mission, vision and values.

But along with how to effectively steward resources through philanthropy, we realized the need to address other critical issues. How can our children manage their finances effectively on a personal level? I believe that sons and daughters who feel confident in their ability to manage their wealth are more likely to have the confidence they need to be generous.

Two Critical Factors

Since I fully understand and appreciate (and have experienced!) the fact that one's children do not always feel eager to listen to their parents, in

2013 we established the first of our quarterly family business meetings. We hired two consultants to advise and educate our children in the basics of financial management and investment. My role was not necessarily to train or to teach, but to keep the family's vision and culture ever present in all of our minds.

As a retired pastor, I began our first meeting with a "devotion" or inspiration (at least I hoped it inspired someone). I wanted to remind our children of two critical factors that will ensure our continued success as we work and plan together.

1. The importance of gratitude

Susie and I have always believed that we were blessed to be a blessing, a phrase you've read throughout this book. The enormous wealth afforded to us did not come our way because of our efforts, but due to the efforts and good fortune of her family.

> The enormous wealth afforded to us did not come our way because of our efforts, but due to the efforts and good fortune of her family.

After emigrating from Sweden, Susie's great grandfather, CJ Segerstrom, decided to relocate from Minnesota to Southern California. He began as a tenant farmer, but in time began to acquire farmland in and around Costa Mesa. Eventually, he had acquired 2,200 acres in Orange County. He had no idea, of course, what Orange County would one day become, nor did he envision that his family would do anything other than farm.

More than half a century later, the state of California decided to build a new freeway connecting the state's coastal cities from Los Angeles to San Diego. Engineers chose to run the new 405 Freeway through southern Orange County, connecting it with the 5 Freeway to San Diego. The new freeway went straight through the middle of the family farm.

Someone in the family had the wisdom and insight to realize that the Segerstroms would not always be farmers, especially with Orange County quickly growing into a bedroom community of Los Angeles. So, the family decided to build what was becoming the new trend in retail: an indoor shopping mall. And thus, South Coast Plaza was born.

Malcolm Gladwell, author of the book *Outliers,* reminds us that no matter how successful one may have become, certain events and incidents have taken place beyond the individual's control that enabled that person to succeed. That's true whether you're Bill Gates or the Beatles. This truth doesn't diminish the hard work and good decisions that also led to their success, but without the good fortune of having a key opportunity, or knowing the right person, or merely being in the right place at the right time, the celebrities of history might never have ascended to their heights of grand achievement.

For this reason, I reminded our children of our family history. If they had no great, great grandfather who bought the land, or no great grandfather who valued it and kept it, or there were no freeway to connect Los Angeles with San Diego—and therefore no easy way to connect South Coast Plaza to thirty prosperous communities—then the Segerstrom name probably would be far less known to local residents than it is. We may owe our good fortune to others, to luck or to divine intervention, but regardless, we need to be thankful. What we enjoy today is *not* just the result of hard work, good decision-making and vision by our ancestors. Still, without the insight of those pioneering family members, we never would be where we are. We are indebted to many people and events beyond our control, and we must always be thankful and appreciative.

2. With privilege comes responsibility
Second, I reminded them that none of us, outside of Susie, are direct descendants of the Segerstrom legacy. We all have been grafted into this family tree either through marriage (like our children's spouses

and me), or adoption (our two children). Since I don't believe much in coincidence, I strive to instill in them the conviction that God has a reason and a purpose for their being part of this family—another way of saying that with great privilege comes great responsibility. They must wisely steward the wealth entrusted to them.

Each family or family member must decide, on his or her own, what that purpose might be. Some see it as payback: they give back to the community or world that so greatly benefited them. Others want to "pay it forward," as in the eponymous movie. They want to inspire others to give as they have been given to. Those with a religious motivation seek to use their wealth in ways that honor their God and bless needy people made in His image.

Family Stewardship

As we strove to become smarter with our philanthropy, we realized that we also needed to prepare our children for stewarding the great wealth that one day will be entrusted to them. When many people hear the word "steward," they think about what they give. But to be a steward or manager also involves serving as a trustee of *what* you keep for your own livelihood or investment.

Never in the history of the United States, or in the world for that matter, has the debate over whether to leave an inheritance to children, or how much one should leave, become so contentious. Those with large estates often fear that leaving heirs too much money would do to them what often happens to big lottery winners—create ultimate failure. Statistics show that 44 percent of all lottery winners have spent their winnings in five years and are twice as likely to declare bankruptcy.

Many parents and grandparents also reason that since they worked hard to amass their wealth, they don't want to deprive their children or grandchildren of the same opportunity. Often, they provide the "seed money" to help their heirs prepare to provide for themselves, either through underwriting their studies or sometimes providing enough to start a business.

As a couple who can fully appreciate the liabilities of bequeathing too much to one's children, we decided that Susie will bequeath a large portion of her inheritance to our son and daughter. Her primary motivation: she did not believe she had the right to end the legacy she had received from her parents, grandparents and great grandparents.

To help mitigate our concerns about overwhelming our children with wealth to the point of self-destruction, we formed a "family office" to support, counsel and train our son and daughter and their spouses for the future management of their inheritance, as well as management of the Family Foundation. The family office consists of the trustee of the family trust and a financial advisor. (From this point on, the term "children" implies both our son and daughter and their spouses.)

Our trustee's primary role is to train our children to become literate in reading financial documents and to create and maintain a budget. He also has the authority to disburse funds from the trust, whenever appropriate. Our financial adviser oversees our family investments (but does not manage them), works on estate strategies, and instructs our children on the intricacies of investing. The trustee begins every session by reviewing the families' various financial statements and teaching our children how to read and understand them. Does employing two advisors add an extra cost? Sure, but their ability to communicate and be listened to, plus training our children, is well worth the cost.

Our financial advisor has three main responsibilities:

➤ To oversee the investments
➤ To equip our children to better understand the investment world
➤ To assist us with our long-term estate strategies.

Finally, we made the important decision to hire a psychologist, Dr. John Townsend, to be our family coach. Since we have virtually married our two children together through the institution of the Dynasty Trust, we deemed it critical to ensure the health, strength and purpose of the family unit. For three years, John worked with us on building and maintaining both our individual and our collective health. He also guided us to achieve an agreed-upon set of core values that will guide our business and foundation activities.

Full Disclosure

When my in-laws were alive, in a manner very typical of their generation, they considered it inappropriate to discuss their estate plan with their children. Nor did they give much thought to preparing their children for their eventual inheritance. You could probably sum up their attitude with this statement: "You are going to get more than enough, and that is all you need to know."

Over the years, I discovered from advisors that most estate plans fail due to a lack of communication between generations. We therefore took the opposite approach and did a "full disclosure" with our children. We revealed everything to them:

- ➤ The full extent of the family's business assets
- ➤ The worth of Mom's portion of the business
- ➤ How much she planned to give and sell to the trust
- ➤ How much she would leave to our foundation.

We believe that such full disclosure will help our children to thrive, even as they grow in their desire and capacity to become wisely generous.

The Dynasty Trust

On the advice of our advisors, in 2012 we implemented a big change to our estate plan. We formed a "dynasty trust," legally known as an "Intentionally Defective Grantor Trust."

Into this trust, we both gifted and sold approximately two-thirds of my wife's interest in the family business. We did this for the benefit of our children and grandchildren, and very possibly for our great grandchildren. The dynasty trust enables us to pass on certain business interests to our heirs without any estate tax. They also will pay no estate tax on the growth of the assets placed within the trust. The dynasty trust also enables us to make distributions to our children and to their families.

When Susie and I first got married, the family's business grew very gradually. Today we see this as a great advantage, since we did not become mesmerized by enormous funds distributed to us and thus had no opportunity to commit great folly. Unlike a lottery winner who receives a windfall in one fell swoop, our income grew gradually, enabling us to become better acclimated to it. We wanted our children to experience the same kind of conditioning we had, rather than to wait many years to receive it all in one big lump sum, when it might have less benefit to their young families. A covenant within the trust places certain conditions upon the receipt of these funds:

> Over the years, I discovered from advisors that most estate plans fail due to a lack of communication between generations.

1. They must maintain full employment. They must remain productive, in whatever career they choose.
2. They must present a budget, and demonstrate an ability to manage that budget, to the satisfaction of the trustee.

We have chosen this path in order to help our children learn how to manage their incomes. We believe that if they are faithful in little, they have a far greater chance of being faithful in much (Luke 16:10).

Growing in Philanthropy

We also strive to train our children in effective philanthropy. Though they have no vote on our foundation's board, they do have an open invitation to sit in on board meetings, have a voice in our grant-making decisions, and participate with our grantees, both here and internationally.

Encouraging your children to internalize great values is as much about modeling those traits as it is about teaching them. As a former pastor, I always said that half a pound of parent was always better than five pounds of pastor. Why? Because we learn best by what is "caught," not taught. We need to model for our children what we want them to learn. That's crucial. If we don't, they will still learn . . . but often the opposite of what we want them to embrace. What we model, they will learn (so we hope).

> Encouraging your children to internalize great values is as much about modeling those traits as it is about teaching them.

Not every child or spouse will display the same amount of interest in giving through a family foundation. The cares of work or family often compete with the demands of running a foundation. People sometimes fail to realize that once you get serious about your giving, it can be like running a small business, with budgets, grants, expenses, planning and travel. Like everything else, it takes time to do well. Young parents and blossoming careers cannot always afford that time.

To better prepare our children for a life of philanthropy, as well as determine their interests and giftedness, we offered to start them with a Donor Advised Fund for their own individual giving. We made the first gift into their fund, and then every contribution they make afterward, up to a certain amount, we have promised to match.

We hope they will continue to display, and even exceed, our generosity. One question now lingers in the back of our minds: Do we maintain the family foundation after our demise, in perpetuity?

The Sunset Clause

Individuals and families who have the capability to continue their philanthropic interests after their lifetimes have given much thought to what's called a "sunset clause." Those who give through a foundation,

Donor Advised Fund or trust whose resources may outlive their lifetime of giving, must face an agonizing decision: should they trust their heirs or trustees to continue to carry out their philanthropic wishes?

We've all heard stories of foundations "gone wrong" or jumping "off the rails" because the heirs or trustees no longer respected the desires and wishes of the principal funder(s). As a couple, Susie and I recognize that possibility, but feel very comfortable that we have a good board, with wise members who have journeyed long with us and who are very knowledgeable of our desires and wishes.

But how long will that team of board members be in place? Will their replacements share the same concerns? Will our children want to remain shackled to *our* vision and mission? What will having an existing family foundation do to their desires and opportunities to give of their own means and resources?

Because of such concerns (and probably several more), many principal funders include a "sunset clause" in their trusts. These clauses stipulate that the foundation or other giving entity will not continue in perpetuity but will expire at some time in the future. Some specify a specific time frame, perhaps five, ten, or twenty years, or at the death of the last member of the generation who willingly continues the principal funder's original philanthropic trajectory.

Many rationales exist for such clauses. If a large sum of money must be distributed after the death of the initial funders—either because a large balance remained in the giving entity, or because of a bequest from the estate—time is needed to wisely steward the distribution of those remaining funds.

In our case, we do not want our children to use our foundation as a substitute for their own giving. We therefore are pondering a sunset clause, not necessarily to put an end to our foundation, but merely to put an end to our funding. We want our children to continue with a work of their own choice, should they choose to go it alone or maintain Sacred Harvest.

One way or another, a sunset is coming. We just want it to be beautiful.

Part Three

Your Journey

Chapter 11

Or My Heart Will Burst

...have the courage to follow your heart and intuition.
They somehow already know what you truly want to become.

STEVE JOBS

A friend of mine entering seminary more than thirty years ago had to take a series of "personality tests," along with everyone else in his incoming class. One of those tests, the MMPI[14], required responses to several hundred statements. Students were asked to rate each statement, indicating where the assertion fell on a scale of "Completely true of me" to "Never true of me." Decades later, my friend still remembers three of those statements:

"My soul often leaves my body."

"My stools are often black."

"I am content with my sex life."

He quickly marked "Never true of me" to the first two statements. But how should he answer the third one? As a single guy who wanted to be married *someday*, how could he say he felt satisfied with his sex life? Would the dean think a sex fiend had walked onto the campus? But if my friend replied, "Never true of me," would the school administration wonder if they had recruited a neurotic loser?

My friend left the question blank.

Personality inventory tests exist because they can provide significant insight into many life situations. I think of the Myers Briggs Type Indicator[15], the DISC Assessment[16], the Big Five assessment[17], the Core Values Index[17] and dozens more. (Do you want to know whether you belong to the House of Slitherin or Griffyndor at the Hogwarts School of Witchcraft and Wizardry? There's a test for that.) Sometimes, however, we remember those tests only where they seemed to go wrong. My friend cannot recall *any* other questions from that massive personality test taken long ago other than the three questions that made him squirm.

Still, as a culture we love these tests. In fact, their seemingly ubiquitous presence reminds me of a wonderful *Dilbert* comic from way back in 1994.

Dogbert, standing in front of Dilbert and other seated employees, says in the first frame, "In 'Diversity Sensitivity' training you will learn to respect those who are different."

In the second frame, he declares, "People basically fall into these four groups," and then shows his audience a typical four quadrant chart— but with a distinct difference. In clockwise order, the first quadrant reads, "Ugly Smart," the second reads "Cute Smart," the third "Cute Stupid" and the last "Ugly Stupid."

In the final frame, Dogbert, now furiously wagging his tail, points to the fourth quadrant and says, "I notice that all of you are in this box."

While I would *never* put you in that fourth box, in my first attempt at writing this chapter, I did create a grid that I eventually abandoned. Let me tell you why.

Not Quite Right

In trying to help you discover what kind of philanthropist you might be, I developed a series of questions. I began my first draft like this:

Only you can write this chapter.

Although I cannot write it for you, I may be able to point you to some good resources from which you can do the heavy lifting (or learning). And make no mistake: thoughtfully answering the question, "who are you?" will take some real time and effort.

So, why is it crucial to know who you are? Knowing yourself is critical because God wants to use you to bless others, especially through the gifts of philanthropy in your near future. God wants to use YOU, with all the abilities, gifts, desires, insights, hopes, experiences and quirks He has built into you. And because we are each a mix of all our experiences, God's plan to use you also includes all of the miscues, fumbles, blunders, gaffes, slip-ups, errors and embarrassments you've committed or endured. He wants to use it all.

He doesn't want you to slavishly follow someone else's path, or fulfill someone else's dream, or mimic someone else's program. If He had wanted that, He could easily have made a world of clones. Did He?

Not by a long shot.

Whatever God wants to do through you, He has in His mind an utterly unique plan. Only you can accomplish it. Only you are called to do it. While you can certainly learn from others, your Creator has little interest in you copying them.

So, adapt more than adopt.

Imagine more than imitate.

Paraphrase more than parrot.

Throughout this book, I've insisted that as a philanthropist, you must walk your own path and find your own road. I've included lots of stories from my own journey, but not because I think anyone should try to reproduce them. We learn best by analogy, by seeing points of similarity and using them to branch out into something new.

Please allow me to insist again: God wants to do something new through you.

What is that new thing? I have no idea. But very often, we can each gain a few clues to the unique path ahead of us by taking a close look at where we've been, what excites us, what interests us, and where we've already enjoyed some success. These are clues, mind you, not road maps. They suggest, they don't stipulate.

So far, so good—but then I wrote this:

In the following pages, I will ask you a long list of questions. I've designed them all to help you answer this one question: "Who are you?" How you answer that question should give you a clearer idea of what a life of philanthropy might look like for you.

As I contemplated the scores of questions I generated, however, something didn't feel quite right. I liked the questions themselves; I thought they could prove invaluable in helping you to discover what sort of philanthropist you might want to become. (For that reason, I've included them as an appendix.) I did not, however, like the way the chapter unfolded.

"Why not?" you might ask. After pondering that very question, I can suggest two reasons.

First, I started thinking of all the great self-tests that already exist (many of them listed earlier in this chapter). Highly intelligent people worked for long periods to develop those tests, and all these instruments can effectively help you get a good handle on how you're wired and where you might "fit." While my questions might assist you to get moving in a helpful direction, these well-established systems can do much more.

But perhaps more importantly, I began thinking in a deeper way about what I had to contribute. Specifically, what could I contribute that these wonderful personality inventories might not? How could I best help you to take your next successful steps on this important journey of philanthropy?

In the end, I still wrote a few key questions . . . but a lot fewer of them. And the four I have created get to the heart of the matter much more quickly.

What Do You Constantly Think About?

Does some vitally important issue, critical need or specific place keep popping into your head? Maybe not a day goes by that your mind doesn't fill up with images of this thing. You don't have to turn your attention in that direction, because your attention never strays far from it.

The Philippines is like that for me, Mindanao in particular. I might be relaxing at home with the TV blaring, but I hardly notice it. Perhaps I vaguely hear a headline about Russia, a story about heart transplants, or reports of genetically engineered corn, or something about lost puppies. I listen, and then…I just go about my business.

But, as soon as I hear the word *Philippines?* My attention races toward the TV. Why? Because my mind never wanders far from that beautiful country and people. I want to quickly know the news of what's happening there. I want to see the tropical storms that hit, or hear of the political developments that roil, or learn about the economic booms or busts shaping this nation that I love. My heart never strays far from the Philippines.

Where is *your* heart? What do you so often find yourself thinking about? What makes your blood pump faster and your mind race more quickly? Whatever *that* is, your core philanthropic interests probably don't trail far behind.

What Do You *Have* to Become?

As you gaze into the future, do you see anything there that you just *have* to become? Perhaps you can't imagine turning the corner into the year 2030 without finding yourself squarely in the center of _____ (fill in the blank).

Zach Hankins knows something of how that feels. He grew up in Charlevoix, Michigan, dreaming of playing Division I basketball. But when Zach broke his foot as a high school senior, he missed nearly the entire season and received exactly *zero* Division I scholarship offers. In fact, he got only one nibble, from Division II Ferris State. The school offered him $3,000 to come and play as a redshirt.

Such a discouraging turn of events might have crushed most players, but not Zach Hankins. He described himself as "very happy to get that opportunity" and parlayed it into an all-American season, where he averaged 15.1 points, 9.7 rebounds and 3.3 blocks per game. Not surprisingly, in 2018 he led Ferris State to the Division II men's basketball championship.

And he was named national Division II Player of the Year.

Xavier head basketball coach Travis Steele took note and offered Hankins a scholarship to join his top tier Division I team. Hankins snapped up the opportunity and immediately started making an impression on his new teammates and coaches.

"Our guys immediately respected Zach," Steel told the *Cincinnati Enquirer.* "He's fearless. He's just that guy: any challenge, he's going to do it. I think that's how he lives his life. That's how he attacks workouts, that's how he attacks conditioning."

"We were doing a treadmill run and I think big guys were at 11.6 miles per hour; they had to do it for a quarter mile. And you know what? Last rep, Zach *increased* the speed to faster than the guards, just to prove a point. That's just kind of who he is. Fearless. He's fit in from day one. I think he's gonna make the most of this opportunity.[19]"

I bet he will! Just listen to Hankins himself: "There's so many talented basketball players who don't get this opportunity or have held themselves back from doing it. I really wanted to take this opportunity because it's a rare one."

Such golden opportunities really are rare—and you have been granted one of the rarest. Not to play Division I basketball, probably, but to make a difference for good on this planet through the gift of wise philanthropy.

Where do you see yourself making such a difference? How do *you* imagine yourself fitting in?

As you contemplate your future in philanthropy, what do you think you just must become?

What Is Your "Holy Discontent"?

I don't know who coined the term "holy discontent," but I do know that former Willow Creek pastor Bill Hybels popularized it. More than a decade ago he wrote a book titled *Holy Discontent: Fueling the Fire that Ignites Personal Vision.*

Hybels' book asked readers to name the one aspect of this broken world that, when they saw it, touched it, or got near it, just set them off. Very likely, the book declared, such a "firestorm of frustration" reflected their holy discontent. In fact, such a growing discontent might disturb them so much that it could throw them "off the couch and into the game."[20]

Do you feel anything like that? Maybe your eyes have been so opened to the needs around you that you feel compelled, even driven, to "do something." Hybels suggests that God might just be whispering to your heart, "I feel the same way about this problem. Now, let's go solve it together!"

If God is calling you to tackle some problem with Him, does that mean it has to be a Big Hairy Audacious Goal, in the terminology of business author Jim Collins?[21] Or if we were to baptize the endeavor a little, would it need to be a Big Holy Audacious Goal? Is that required, if God is involved?

Hardly. I would say, don't worry if your "holy discontent" is not a BHAG. Most BHAGs that I know of usually seem more ego-driven rather than God-driven. For that reason, I've never been a big fan of viewing them as a motivational necessity. We must never forget these words commonly attributed to Mother Teresa: "Not all of us can do great things. But we can do small things with great love."[22] Do you see the great wisdom there? In fact, God does not call us all to do great things, but He does call us all to love greatly.

In the Bible, God called some heroes to do great and mighty things, while He called others to do small and barely whispered things. Both did what they could, and both are part of God's great narrative.

> In the Bible, God called some heroes to do great and mighty things, while He called others to do small and barely whispered things.

Does some "holy discontent" disturb your sleep at night? Do you feel a rush of "righteous irritation" every time you read a news story or watch a documentary about some glaring social need? When you think of a particular community, or of a region in your part of the country, or of a needy nation across the seas, do the challenges there make you want to call out, "Why doesn't somebody *do* something about that?"

Could you be that "somebody"?

"If I Don't Do *This*, My Heart Will Burst"

Perhaps I could fit all these questions into one tidy little package. Does some need, challenge, problem or difficulty so trouble or even rile you that the neurons in your brain keep flowing in that direction? Perhaps you feel compelled to do what you can, and sometimes you even think, *If I don't do this, my heart will burst!*

If that sounds anything like you, then you're probably close to finding your philanthropic Holy Grail. Or at least, you may be well on your way.

Todd Henry, blogging about men and women finding their career "sweet spot," wrote:

> Your sweet spot is discovered through active contemplation, not passive reflection. The broader your base of experience, the more patterns you will be able to discern. Some people think that their sweet spot should be obvious, and as a result

they waste a lot of time trying to "find their passion" or figure out their optimal career path before diving in. Instead, great contributors begin by adding value wherever they can, then spend time sorting the results later. [23]

I consider that pretty sound advice. I also like what Henry says next. Even though it pertains specifically to work, I believe it applies equally to philanthropy:

> "Passion" does not necessarily translate to "comfort," or even to "pleasure".

> Many people think that once they discern their sweet spot, work will be perpetual bliss. Not so. Often, the place where you are most effective requires doing something that you don't find personally thrilling, but that allows you to have massive impact. I know many prolific writers who – gasp! – don't enjoy the process of writing, and many great entrepreneurs who find building a team a bit of a grind. However, they also recognize that they are uniquely capable of adding value through these activities, and they are more in love with the results than they are with their temporary comfort.

Henry is right. "Passion" does not necessarily translate to "comfort," or even to "pleasure" (in the ordinary sense of the term). It does, however, habitually lead to both effectiveness and good results. And that's a pretty good segue to my closing thought.

The Call of the Creator

Throughout the Bible, we see men and women being "called" by God to serve in this or that capacity. Sometimes the Scripture uses the term "call," although many times it simply describes how God led or directed individuals to do certain tasks at certain times in certain places.

The one aspect all of these incidents have in common is variety, even extreme variety. Sometimes these human servants, such as Moses,

Samuel, Elijah, and Paul, heard an audible divine voice. Other times, God directed men and women—Joseph, Rahab, and Esther, to name a few—through circumstances or unusual opportunities. At still other times, men and women "heard" the voice of God through prophets, apostles, or other believers. A pagan seer named Balaam even heard God's voice through the mouth of his donkey (Numbers 22:21-39)!

So, what does this biblical history have to do with philanthropy today?

God often called men and women to missions that seem very far from a natural fit.

All too often, I suspect we err badly when we suppose that our "true calling" *always* relates to our giftedness and our passion. The problem is that in the scriptural accounts, God often called men and women to missions that seem very far from a natural fit. A few examples:

➤ Moses did *not* see himself as a national deliverer of thousands of Israelites.
➤ Jonah did *not* see himself preaching to his nation's enemy, the Ninevites.
➤ Ananias did *not* see himself buddying up to Saul (who later became Paul the apostle).
➤ Peter did *not* see himself helping Gentiles to come to Jesus.

None of these men pictured themselves involved in any of these ways, but God clearly called each of them specifically to their critical missions.

God works through our passions, yes; but He is never constrained by them.

Sometimes, He intends to accomplish more through us outside of our passions and interests than He could within them.

By all means, discover your passion! Learn how you're wired! Ponder where you've had success! Listen to people who might see things more clearly than you do!

But never forget that God may choose you for tasks that have never once entered your head.

One Clear Truth

Perhaps the only clear-cut truth here is that God takes great delight in choosing us to fulfill a purpose we cannot always understand. As my friend, John Townsend, writes in his book, *Leading from Your Gut,* "sometimes calling precedes passion."[24]

Indeed, it does.

While nearly every great leader has both gifts and passion, the biblical saints teach us that even gifts and passion ultimately must bend the knee to God's call. Gifts and passion, while important, are never ultimate.

So, do gifts and passion count for nothing if God chooses to call us in a different direction? Well, I didn't say that, either.

As we step out in faith and obedience, God frequently births in us a new passion, something that didn't exist in our hearts before. Eventually, new gifts also burst onto the scene, whether developed in us or provided through another. Moses had his brother, Aaron. The Apostle Paul had his friend Barnabas (and later, Silas). ...How is one possibly to discern God's voice amidst the noise? Buechner offers some advice:

> "By and large a good rule for finding out is this: the kind of work God usually calls you to is the kind of work (a) that you need most to do and (b) that the world most needs to have done. ... The place God calls you to is the place where your deep gladness and the world's deep hunger meet" (118-19).[25]

So where does God want to use you in this wonderful, wild, and sometimes wacky world of wise philanthropy? I have no idea. You may not, either (at least, not yet).

But so what? Someone Else does.

And He has a way of making sure His calls get through.

Chapter 12

Why Give?

For it is in giving that we receive.

FRANCIS OF ASSISI

Americans are a generous people.

A 2016 report by the Charities Aid Foundation (headquartered in the UK) named the United States as the most generous nation on earth, followed by New Zealand and Canada. Americans won the accolade by displaying the highest rate of charitable donations as a percentage of their country's gross domestic product.[26]

In 2017, Americans donated an estimated $410 *billion* dollars to charity, an increase of 5.2 percent over the previous year. Giving by foundations went up an estimated 6 percent, corporate giving increased by 8 percent, and giving by bequest rose 2.3 percent. Per capita giving by adults reached $1,165, while the average U.S. household gave $2,271 to charity. [27]

That's a lot of giving!

And where did all that charitable giving go? As you might expect, it went to a blizzard of causes and groups, from environment/animals (3 percent) to arts, culture and humanities (5 percent) to health (9 percent) to education (14 percent) to religion (the largest segment, at 31 percent).

Compared to other nations, Americans give a lot of their money each year to charitable organizations. But *why* do they give? What motivates them to reach into their pocketbooks and hand over a chunk of their wealth to this or that cause or organization?

I ask, because as philanthropists, donors and grant-givers, you and I really need to know. We want to encourage others to join us in this journey toward wise generosity. If we know some of the key reasons why people give, then perhaps we can improve our own efforts at encouraging others to join us in working together to make the world a better place.

A World of Motivations

It turns out there are as many reasons to give as there are charities to give to. The "science of charity" really took off in the late 1990s[28], and much of that period's research culminated in a 2010 book called *The Science of Giving: Experimental Approaches to the Study of Charity*, by Daniel Oppenheimer and Christopher Olivola. Their book, based on many ground-breaking experiments by several independent researchers, offers a number of surprising revelations.

Giving to individuals vs giving to groups

Did you know, for example, that people tend to give far more money to suffering individuals than they do to *groups* of hurting people? That may seem counterintuitive. Shouldn't we want to help more people than fewer of them? Maybe . . . and yet, if you "tell donors about even two hungry children, or give them statistics about hungry children generally," do you know what happens? "Donations will fall by half."[29]

As you move further into this journey, therefore, I'd strongly encourage you to collect great stories along the way. People have a far greater tendency to respond to true life stories that you tell with personal passion, than they do to slick presentations filled with statistics, pleas and pie charts. Sometimes, those stories might even explain why *you* give.

About six years ago we were in Davao, Mindanao, Philippines, interviewing potential grantees. For two days, we kept encountering grant requests that asked for funds equal to 90 percent of the organization's total grant budget, from $80,000 to $120,000. By this time, Sacred Harvest had been in the country for six or seven years, and we were becoming a known entity. But I started to wonder: Were we becoming known merely as a "charitable bank?" Did the faith-based NGO world see us only as an ATM machine?

In that moment, whatever enjoyment I had received from getting to work with and learning about other ministries had vanished. I felt both angry and used.

And then one of our previous partners brought to us a younger couple, former Muslims who had become followers of Isa (Jesus in Arabic). Our friend had been mentoring them. I learned that because of their newfound faith, their village had ostracized them. In response, and with their own money, they opened a little pre-school to serve the children of the village. In time, the village had welcomed them back into the community.

The building the couple used as a school employed typical Filipino construction: wood and woven bamboo for walls. This meant that when the rains came (a weekly occurrence in most of Mindanao), strong winds blew sheets of rain into the classroom, soaking students and teachers alike. This couple came to us requesting only $3,000 so they could give the classroom some windows.

I wept inside.

Here before me stood a dedicated young couple, trying to live out in their Muslim village the life of a Jesus follower . . . and using their own money to serve. They wanted only a small sum to make life a little more comfortable for the children.

Do you think I wanted to give to that couple? It was a slam dunk. They got their grant, not because of its small size, but because we wanted to honor them for their faithful, sacrificial service. We even added an extra $2,000, because we felt sure they had more they could accomplish; they needed to report only how they would use the extra funds.

Poignant stories like this one can rightly motivate people to give. They certainly do that for me! What else motivates people to give?

The motivation of pain

Strangely, pain can move some men and women to give, but probably not in the way you suppose. Have you ever taken part in a fund raiser in which a participant had to do something painful in order to attract donations, such as run a marathon? Science has discovered that "when people anticipate that they're going to have to suffer to raise money for a charity, then their willingness to contribute to that cause actually goes up."[30]

Pain can motivate people to philanthropy in other ways, too. One of the most respected non-profit organizations in the world, Mothers Against Drunk Driving (MADD) got its start in 1980. Candace Lightner began the group in May after her thirteen-year-old daughter, Cari, was killed in a hit-and-run accident involving a drunk driver. The man had been arrested four times previously for driving under the influence. Candace's pain drove her to start a highly effective group that claims to have helped save more than 330,000 lives since Cari's death.

Sometimes, we mistakenly think that we need to clear away all barriers if we are to "grease the skids" for donations, convinced that we should make the process as pain-free as possible. But that does not appear to be true.

As I pondered this science-based insight, I started to hear the words of King David, ringing in my ears. David wanted to acquire a special piece of land, on which Israel could build its first temple. The owner of the land offered to give it to the king, free and clear—and David replied, "No, I insist on paying the full price. I will not take for the Lord what is yours or sacrifice a burnt offering that costs me nothing" (1 Chronicles 21:24, NIV). I doubt the king was especially unusual here. Most of us have little interest in giving trivial gifts in the name of some great cause.

The motivation of self-protection

What else motivates people to give? Frankly, some motivations for giving don't excite me much. Israeli psychologist Tehila Kogut teaches at Ben Gurion University of the Negev. Her work suggests that people sometimes give to charity to protect themselves.

Suppose an organization calls a prospective donor. When the person doesn't recognize the phone number, he or she likely will ignore the call, rather than pick up the phone and tell the solicitor "no." Why? Well, suppose the caller is trying to raise money for cancer research. "They feel that if they say no," Kogut said, "the probability that they will have cancer will increase, that this is an act of tempting fate."[31] For such people, giving becomes an attempt to avoid personal catastrophe.

I'm not at all sure I want to encourage people to give so that bad karma doesn't put them in a coffin. And I have no interest in motivating them to become generous so that they don't get leukemia. Maybe there's a way to use this motivation for God-honoring and people-loving purposes, but I can't think of one. Maybe you can do better?

The motivation of a "warm glow"

I know that one often-cited motivation for giving really does "work." James Andreoni, an economics professor at the University of California at San Diego, in 1989 proposed what he called the "warm glow" theory. It suggests that some people give because of the personal pleasure they feel in knowing they've contributed to a good cause. I know this motivation "works," because I've seen it work in me.

In our fifth year of grant making in Mindanao, two lovely Filipinas walked into our board room to describe their mission. They did a fine job of presenting their grant proposal, its vision and goal. Once every month, they set out about five a.m. and kept walking until 9 p.m., when they reached a tribal group they discipled in the mountains of central Mindanao. As they spoke, we could tell they made a sacrificial effort to serve. Unfortunately, they often got forgotten or ignored by the churches that sponsored them. The youngest of the pair, about twenty-seven years old, told us how she had miscarried on one of these trips.

My heart broke as I listened. My wife and I had experienced five miscarriages during our marriage. I just wanted to hug both women and pray for them.

But then God brought to mind a question that would become invaluable in serving future grantees. "What can we do for you?" I asked.

The women immediately began to list all the things their ministry could use. I stopped them.

"What I mean is, what do you need?" I asked.

Both women began to weep. No one had ever bothered to ask them such a question. They then told us how they and their spouses had to sacrifice just to keep the mission going.

We not only approved their grant request, but we decided to honor both of them and their spouses with a "love gift" to be used for their own needs, perhaps even a dinner out. Did that gift give me a "warm glow"? Indeed, it did. Has it helped to motivate me to give at other times? I'm sure it has.

That's one of the delightful things about giving from the heart: Not only do you get to help someone in need, but you get the pleasure of seeing their lives improve. I believe that the best altruism sparks real joy from the good it does. "Dispassionate benevolence" may sound impressive in theory, but it falls flat. I would much rather follow God's example, who once said of his people, "I will rejoice in doing them good and will assuredly plant them in this land with all my heart and soul" (Jeremiah 32:41, NIV).

> That's one of the delightful things about giving from the heart: Not only do you get to help someone in need, but you get the pleasure of seeing their lives improve.

Three Main Categories

Scientific explanations for why people choose to donate to charitable causes tend to cluster in three categories:

➤ *Purely altruistic:* The supporter values the social good supplied by the charity.

➤ *Impurely altruistic:* The supporter gains personal value from knowing he/she supported the charity.

➤ *Non-altruistic:* The supporter wants to show off. (Or maybe just get a tax write off.)

Reporter Phyllis Korkki of *The New York Times* explained that while some people do give for personal recognition, they represent only a small subset of the population. Such people feel it's important to express their moral values to others. Individuals with a strong set of internalized moral values, however, such as those with strong religious convictions, typically don't need the promise of future recognition.[32]

Michael Sanders and Francesca Tamma have reported several other fascinating reasons why people give. In a 2015 article titled, "The science behind why people give to charity," they listed several of these reasons, including:[33]

➤ If someone helps another person write a will, and merely asks if the person would like to donate, the individual is more likely to consider it. In fact, the rate of donation roughly doubles.

➤ Advertisements boasting the proven effectiveness of a charity do not increase giving; in fact, they can have the opposite effect.

➤ Giving is fundamentally a social act. People give significantly more to their *alma mater,* for example, if the person asking for a donation is a former roommate.

➤ When donors see that someone before them has made a large donation, they make a larger donation themselves.

➤ Donors are more likely to respond to a matching-fund campaign if they know that the match comes from a well-known entity (such as the Bill and Melinda Gates Foundation) than if it comes from an anonymous source.

➤ Celebrity endorsements increase donations to charity very quickly, but apparently only with individuals who already have donated to the charity.

Several studies have shown that charitable giving "is contagious; seeing others give makes an individual more likely to give. Gentle encouragement from a prominent person in your life can make a big difference to your donation decisions, more than quadrupling them."[34]

This may be part of the reason why "matching" challenges can work so well. Giving really can become contagious.

We got a visit once from a group of master's-degreed pastors who had left an urban Bible school to relocate to a very remote mountain Bible School, hoping to "salvage" it. A US missionary had begun the distant school fifty years before to serve indigenous people, but it had nearly died. We saw pictures of an old, wooden Bible school building with floors ready to collapse and classrooms open to the region's frequent rains.

The young pastors presented a grant proposal for funds to repair their building, but without money for a toilet (they feared they already had reached the maximum allowed grant). In the course of our interview, we discovered they had at least one meager income source: they ran a small farm, donated by a retired faculty member. Proceeds from the farm augmented the needs of current faculty and supplemented "tuition" from impoverished students yearning to study well so they could reach their communities for Christ.

Our board approved a grant, but also challenged the pastors to raise money for building two toilets. We said that any amount they raised for this purpose, we would match with an additional grant. They accepted the challenge and quickly produced the amount needed.

Not surprisingly, perhaps, science has found that habit also plays a part in giving. Those who have volunteered before are more likely to donate their time than those who have never volunteered. This suggests that if you want people to join you in giving, you might first invite them to join you in volunteering. Get them in a habit, and then see where it leads.

One last finding of science doesn't surprise me at all. "Spending money on others actually makes us happier than spending it on ourselves," claims this discovery by Sanders and Tamma, "and giving to others can actually make us healthier."[35]

Suppose Susie and I had never chosen to start Sacred Harvest. Suppose we had never gone down the charitable giving route at all. Suppose that as her family's business grew, we simply kept for ourselves the millions it generated. Do you think we would be happier today? Do you think we would be healthier? I doubt it. My work with Sacred Harvest gives me as much joy as any job I've ever had, and perhaps more. And had we spent all that money on ourselves, I can easily imagine I'd have eaten or indulged my way into the hospital by now. I can therefore wholeheartedly endorse an ancient saying: "A generous person will prosper; whoever refreshes others will be refreshed" (Proverbs 11:25).

The Heart Does More

As I scanned all the reasons science and the Internet offer for why people give, I observed at least one "truism" reflected in both sources. Here's the truth:

The heart does more than the head to motivate us charitable giving.

We can show men and women all the graphs, statistics, pie charts and numbers that we want, but a far higher percentage of them will give for emotional reasons than for informational ones. One website advised donation-seeking charities not to neglect three major considerations:[36]

➢ People act from the heart, not the head
➢ Giving is a personal act
➢ The act of giving is immediate

The website also advised its readers, "Your appeals need to be donor-centric. Make sure to tell your donor why they should care, and why they matter to your organization. Give your donors the opportunity to act here and now. Your relationship with them will be long-term, but their willingness to give is now—let them act on it."

As you ponder your own journey toward wise generosity, I'd encourage you to spend some time thinking about these three highlighted bits of counsel. Turn those three words over in your mind: *Heart. Personal. Immediate.* How can a focus on those three things help you to encourage others to join you in the task ahead?

What I've Observed

Generous people tend to be happier people, and the size of an individual's wealth has nothing to do with their joy. I know wealthy people who never seem to have enough, and I've also seen an amazing spirit of contentment among the generous poor.

Some give out of a conviction that they have a social responsibility; they have been given much, and they want to give back a portion of what they possess.

A life tragedy can become a catalyst for someone deciding to address the social, physical, emotional and spiritual needs of society.

Even guilt and shame can motivate some to give (although usually not for very long).

Strategic or heartfelt causes can lift people's aspirations to give.

Some express a need to make a difference in some area of human experience.

People with a strong religious faith often feel a compulsion to help. If they are Christians, they likely will cite Bible verses such as the following:

> Give, and it will be given to you. A good measure, pressed
> down, shaken together and running over, will be poured into
> your lap. For with the measure you use, it will be measured to
> you. (Luke 6:38, NIV)

Each of you should give what you have decided in your heart to give, not reluctantly or under compulsion, for God loves a cheerful giver. (2 Corinthians 9:7, NIV)

Although some individuals have a strong preference for giving anonymously, others believe that by making known their involvement, more individuals can be inspired to give. A friend of mine calls this "tithing your influence."

The truth is, motives for generous giving range from selfless to totally self-serving, and everywhere in between. While meditating on this wild assortment of reasons for giving can help us in our charitable work and as we ponder how to encourage more people to "get in the game," we can't afford to forget the most important question of all:

> Why do I want to get involved in philanthropy? What are my reasons for giving?

Why do I want to get involved in philanthropy? What are my reasons for giving?

Generosity Is the Thing

On one level, I suppose it doesn't make much of a difference why you want to "get in the game." The world and its people need help, and you've been granted the opportunity to give. In one way, a dollar given selfishly is no different than a dollar given selflessly; they'll both buy someone a dollar's worth of help.

In another way, though, it matters a great deal why you give. A selfish person rarely gives generously, and generosity is the thing I'm trying to encourage. I did not set out to write a book called *A Journey Toward Selfish Generosity*.

So . . . why do *you* give?

I think it's important that you know, because the answer will shape the rest of your journey. It will influence and even determine the kind of generosity you express with your life. I want to promote smarter generosity, and the *why* greatly influences how smart we can become.

As I wrap up this little book, I am not going to sermonize. I am not going to lecture. I won't warn, chide, plead, flatter, wheedle, cajole, admonish or argue. I'm just going to follow the lead of my boss, who often ended His presentations with a question hanging in the air. So, here's my question:

Why do *you* give?

Appendix A

Recommended Reading

Brest, Paul and Hal Harvey. (2008.) *Money Well Spent: A Strategic Plan for Smart Philanthropy.* Bloomberg Press.

Buzzotta, Lefton, Cheney and Beatty. (1998). *Making Common Sense Common Practice.* New York: Psychological Associates Inc.

Callahan, David and Alfred A. Knoff. (2017). *The Givers: Wealth, Power, and Philanthropy in a New Gilded Age.* New York: Penguin Random House.

Corbett, Steve and Brian Fickert. (2014). *When Helping Hurts: How to Alleviate Poverty without Hurting the Poor...and Yourself.* Chicago: Moody Publishers.

George, Bill. (2003). *Authentic Leadership*. San Francisco: Jossey Bass.

Hybels, Bill. (2008). *Holy Discontent: Fueling the Fire that Ignites Personal Vision*. Grand Rapids: Zondervan.

Jernigan, Don. (2016). *The Hidden Power of Relentless Stewardship: 5 Keys to Developing a World-Class Organization*. New York: Rosetta Books.

Livermore, David A. (2012). *Serving with Eyes Wide Open: Doing Worldwide Missions with Cultural Intelligence*. Ada, MI: Baker Book House.

Lupton, Robert (2011). *Toxic Charity: How Churches and Charities Hurt Those They Help, and How to Reverse It*. New York: HarperCollins Books.

Macaulay, David (1988). *The Way Things Work*. Boston: Houghton Mifflin.

Macaulay, David (2016). *The Way Things Work Now*. Boston: Houghton Mifflin Harcourt and Dorling Kindserley.

Stern, Kenneth (2013). *With Charity for All: Why Charities are Failing and a Better Way to Give*. New York: Doubleday.

Townsend, John (2018). *Leading from Your Gut*. Grand Rapids: Zondervan.

Appendix B

Popular Giving Vehicles

A comparison of donor-advised funds, supporting organizations, and private foundations

ISSUE / FEATURE	DONOR-ADVISED FUNDS	SUPPORTING ORGANIZATIONS	PRIVATE FOUNDATIONS
Description of the giver's role and Governance	Givers have advisory privileges only. Ultimate control rests with the public charity.	Neither the giver nor a family member can control, directly or indirectly, more than 49% of the board, but the giver may participate in the selection of board members.	The giver family can control 100% of the board; however, after the giver's death, the board has control.
Control over grants and assets	The giver may recommend grants and investment options, but the public charity has ultimate control over decisions.	The giver may recommend grants and investments, but the board of the SO has ultimate control over decisions.	The board has complete control of all grants and investment decisions, subject to self-dealing rules.
Tax deduction limits for gifts of cash and publicly-traded securities	Cash: 60% of adjusted gross income; publicly-traded securities: 30% of adjusted gross income	Cash: 60% of adjusted gross income; publicly-traded securities: 30% of adjusted gross income	Cash: 30% of adjusted gross income; publicly-traded securities: 20% of adjusted gross income
Tax deduction limits for other non-liquid appreciated assets (long-term capital gain)	Fair market value up to 30% of adjusted gross income	Fair market value up to 30% of adjusted gross income	Lesser of fair market value or the giver's basis in asset up to 20% of adjusted gross income
Investment excise taxes	None	None	Must pay tax on investment income
Distribution requirements	None	None	5% of foundation assets must be distributed annually
Start-up costs[1]	None	Legal and state fees for incorporation, IRS filing, and other documents (no IRS filing if under NCF group exemption)	Legal and state fees for incorporation, IRS filing, and other documents
Ongoing administrative and management costs[1]	It varies depending on the public charity providing the service ... generally 1% per year or less.	Ongoing fees for accounting, legal, and administrative advisors to oversee the assets, balance the books, pay the bills, keep the records, and file the tax returns	Ongoing fees for accounting, legal, and administrative advisors to oversee the assets, balance the books, pay the bills, keep the records, and file the tax returns
Ability to employ people and pay salaries and benefits	No	Yes, subject to reasonable compensation limits; no to substantial contributors[2]	Yes, subject to reasonable compensation limits
Ability to pay expenses for travel/other reimbursements	No	Yes, able to pay expenses but not able to reimburse expenses to substantial contributors[2]	Yes
Ability to make grants to non-exempt individuals	No	Yes, subject to the same requirements as grants to foreign charitable organizations	Yes, subject to the same requirements as grants to foreign charitable organizations
Anonymity of giver	Yes	No[3]	No[3]
Privacy	Complete privacy is available. DAF information is aggregated with other DAF information to maintain privacy, and an individual tax return is not required for each DAF.	The entity must file Form 990, which becomes a matter of public record and contains detailed information on grants, investment fees, salaries, etc.[3]	The entity must file Form 990 which becomes a matter of public record and contains detailed information on grants, investment fees, salaries, etc.[3]
Succession and Perpetuity	Can exist in perpetuity	Can exist in perpetuity	Can exist in perpetuity

1.   The creation of any legal entity, especially one that could last in perpetuity and/or involves irrevocable actions, requires the careful input and oversight of a competent attorney that has a thorough understanding of the giver's family and their giving goals and objectives.

2.   Substantial contributors are defined in IRC § 507(d)(2)(A).

3.   Combining this tool with a donor-advised fund (NCF Giving Fund) can achieve partial privacy and anonymity.

* Information in this chart is based on federal laws as of the date of this printing. These laws are subject to change and can affect the accuracy of this information.

Appendix C

Questions to Help You on Your Way

If you would like a little "boost" on your way to discovering where you might realize the biggest impact in your life of philanthropy, the following questions may be helpful to you. I have organized the questions that follow into six broad categories:

➤ Background
➤ Gifting
➤ Training
➤ Interests
➤ Goals
➤ Calling

While most of these categories have some connection with one another, they also differ from each other in significant ways. By the time you finish reflecting upon and answering these questions, I hope you will find yourself better equipped to start walking down a smarter path to a life of generosity.

Your Background

1. Describe the home in which you grew up. What "life lessons" did you learn there?

2. Who were your three best friends as a child? As a teen? What drew you to them?

3. Where did you experience the most success as a child? As an adolescent? As a young adult?

4. What shaped you the most in your formative years? Who had the greatest influence on you? Why?

5. Pick a single word to describe your background. Why did you choose this word?

6. Describe the single greatest experience of your life so far. What made this experience "great"?

7. Describe the single worst or hardest experience of your life so far. Why was it so difficult for you?

8. What do you value most about your background? What do you value least? Why?

9. Name a teacher who had a strong influence or effect on you, whether good or bad. How does that teacher's influence continue to influence you now?

10. If you had a time machine and could return to any moment in your life—but only as an observer—to what moment in your past would you return? Why?

Your Gifting

1. Name what you consider to be your three top gifts, strengths, talents or traits. Where do you shine?

2. Ask the person closest to you—your spouse, friend, co-worker, family member—to identify what he or she views as your top three gifts. (No coaching!) Do your lists match? Are they close? What can you glean from this comparison?

3. Describe the sense of pleasure or satisfaction you get from using

your top three gifts.

4. What have these gifs enabled you to accomplish so far?

5. How do others tend to rely on your gifts? What are you often asked to do?

6. Name the two or three most memorable compliments you have received from people who praised you for using your gifts effectively.

7. Think of a time or place when you wanted to use your gifts but couldn't. What stopped you? How did that experience make you feel?

8. Think about the future: Where and how would you like to use your gifts? (Don't limit your imagination!)

9. Think about how your gifts engage or connect well with the gifts of others. Where have you seen your gifts complement those of others? Where have you seen them clash with others?

10. How have you honed your gifts? Where do they still need more sharpening?

Your Training

1. What subjects did you like in school? What subjects did you hate? Why?

2. What special training have you received that continues to help you succeed?

3. In what areas of school did you excel? Where did you struggle?

4. If you attended college, what kind of training did you receive there? Have you remained in the field for which you trained? Why or why not? If you didn't attend college, name the most helpful training you received as a young adult. What made this training so exceptional?

5. Name an area in which you'd still like to get some training. Why do you want it? How might it help you? How could you get the training you desire? For what purpose would you use it?

6. What sort of training, formal or informal, has most helped you to succeed in your current career? What made this training so effective or helpful?

7. Describe your learning style. What helps you learn most effectively? How quickly do you learn? What kind of learning process is challenging for you? Do people generally like to have you as a student? Are you "teachable?" Explain or give examples.

8. Describe yourself as a trainer. Who have you trained? In what have you trained them? Do you think they learned well from you as a trainer? Did they enjoy learning from you? Explain.

9. Imagine yourself in ten years. How has your life training equipped you to be an effective philanthropist? Where might you still be struggling in a decade? What kind of training could you get today that could help you years from now?

Your Interests

1. List your five top interests in regard to your job or career.

2. List your five top interests that are *not* related to your work.

3. On your "average work day," which of your activities or responsibilities is most enjoyable or interesting to you? Why? Which activities do you enjoy the least? Why?

4. On your days off, what do you most enjoy doing, and why do you enjoy it?

5. Outside of your work, if you could spend a year doing one thing, what would it be? Why?

6. Do you enjoy reading? What do you like reading about in your spare time?

7. If you ran an international media conglomerate, what topics would you choose as your focus to highlight? Why?

8. Think of the most fulfilling moment you experienced in the past month. What were you doing? Why did you find the experience to be so fulfilling?

9. What causes you to smile, without fail? What gets your blood pumping (outside of exercise)? What would you give a million dollars to be a part of?

10. Describe your most common daydreams. What hopes or dreams just keep coming back to you?

Your Goals

1. What would you like to accomplish in the next five years?
2. What would you like to accomplish in the next ten years?
3. What do you hope to have accomplished by the end of your life?
4. Name a personal goal that you have yet to reach. What has kept you from reaching that goal?
5. Identify three purposes or goals that you'd like to accomplish through your philanthropy.
6. Name a career goal that you seem close to reaching. How did you get to this point?
7. Maybe, like Steve, you tend to have more "directions" than "goals." What current directions interest you the most? Why?
8. Think about the kind of philanthropy you *might* want to pursue. Identify one short-term goal (within one month), a medium-term goal (within six months) and a long-term goal (within one year) that could help you to determine what kind of projects or needs you'd like to learn more about or pursue.
9. Whom do you know who actively pursues some philanthropic interests? Invite the person out for coffee, explaining that you'd like to learn about his or her goals for giving. What, specifically, do they want to accomplish through their philanthropy?
10. Describe your current overall goal for your giving, regardless of how formed or unformed it might be. What would you like to accomplish?

Your Calling

1. A calling can be described as a strong desire for a particular way of life or vocation. What does "calling" mean to you?

2. A "calling" implies being chosen or requested by someone, a value or some force. If you believe you have a calling, who is the one, force, or value that is calling you? Explain.

3. Do you believe you have a philanthropic "calling"? If so, what is it? If not, do you wish you had one? Explain.

4. Interview someone you know who has mentioned their own "calling." Find out all you can about this calling: What it is, how they got or discovered it, how it motivates them, whether it grows or changes, how it helps them direct their activities, etc.

5. Consider reading the book *The Call: Finding and Fulfilling the Central Purpose of Your Life,* by Os Guinness (2003). If you read the book, describe your chief take-away from it.

6. How do you believe a clear sense of a personal calling would benefit you as you pursue a life of generosity?

7. The Bible frequently uses the word "calling" ("called," "calls") to speak about God's plans for a person's life. Describe what the following New Testament text means to you:

    ". . . we constantly pray for you, that our God may make you worthy of his calling, and that by his power he may bring to fruition your every desire for goodness and your every deed prompted by faith" (2 Thessalonians 1:11).

8. Describe what the following quote by Charles Swindoll means to you:

    "When you have a sense of calling, whether it's to be a musician, soloist, artist, in one of the technical fields, or a plumber, there is something deep and enriching when you realize it isn't just a casual choice, it's a divine calling."[37]

9. How would a sense of "calling" affect the application of the following quote by Bill Gates?

> "Effective philanthropy requires a lot of time and creativity—the same kind of focus and skills that building a business requires."[38]

10. Invest some time in thinking about your own calling, its nature or even its possibility. Then, in the space below, write a concise statement of your personal calling—or if you're not sure you have one, a concise statement of what a personal calling for you *might* look like:

Once you've worked through all of the preceding questions (and a few exercises), try to synthesize your answers into a brief, working statement of who you are. Write that statement below.
This is who I am:

Now, here's the *vital* question: What might a life of generosity look like for a person who describes him/herself as you have just written? Where could such a person most satisfyingly begin to walk a journey of smarter philanthropy?

That is the chapter you need to write.
Start *today.*

Endnotes

1   Gates, Mary. "Bill Gates' mother inspired philanthropy." Business Insider, 10 May 2015. https://www.businessinsider.com/bill-gates-mother-inspired-philanthropy-2015-5/?r=SPH&IR=T. Accessed 13 Nov 2018.

2   "benchmarking." *BusinessDictionary,* 5 Dec. 2018, http://www.businessdictionary.com/definition/benchmarking.html.

3,   Ben Bloch, "Chip Kelly takes the fast track to tremendous heights at Oregon before hitting speed bumps in the NFL."

4.   Bill George, *Authentic Leadership* (San Francisco: Jossey Bass, 2003), 63.

5.   "Pursuing your Philanthropic Vision." US Trust, www.ustrust.com/articles/pursuing-your-philanthropic-vision.html.

6. Don Jernigan, *The Hidden Power of Relentless Stewardship: 5 Keys to Developing a World-Class Organization* (New York: Rosetta Books, 2016), 74.

7. Buzzotta, Lefton, Cheney and Beatty. *Making Common Sense Common Practice.* New York: Psychological Associates Inc., 1998.

8. Rita Gunther McGrath and Ian MacMillan, "Discovery-Driven Planning," *Harvard Business Review,* July-August 1995.

9. "Peter Principle." *Investopedia.com.* https://www.investopedia.com/terms/p/peter-principle.asp. Accessed Nov 26, 2018.

10. Lupton, Robert D. *Toxic Charity: How Churches and Charities Hurt Those They Help (And How to Reverse It).* Harper Collins Publishers, 2002.

11. Livermore, David. *Serving with Eyes Wide Open.* Baker Publishing Group, 2012.

12. Fikkert, Brian and Steve Corbett. *When Helping Hurts: Alleviating Poverty without Hurting the Poor—and Yourself.* Moody Publishers, 2009.

13. Lupton, Robert. *Charity Detox: What Charity Would Look Like if We Cared about Results.* HarperOne, 2015. Moody Publishers, 2009.

14. Minnesota Multiphasic Personality Inventory. https://www.verywellmind.com/what-is-the-minnesota-multiphasic-personality-inventory-2795582

15. https://en.wikipedia.org/wiki/Myers%E2%80%93Briggs_Type_Indicator

16. https://en.wikipedia.org/wiki/DISC_assessment

17. ttps://en.wikipedia.org/wiki/Big_Five_personality_traits

18. https://consciousendeavors.org/core-values-index/

19. Adam Baum, "Xavier basketball grad transfer Zach Hankins: 'I never thought I'd get here.'" Sept. 21, 2018. https://www.cincinnati.com/story/sports/college/xavier/xaviersports/2018/09/21/xavier-basketball-grad-transfer-zach-hankins-never-thought-id-get-here/1344484002/

20. Hybels, Bill. *Holy Discontent: Fueling the Fire that Ignites Personal Vision.* Zondervan, 2008.

21. Collins, Jim. https://www.jimcollins.com/concepts/bhag.html

22. https://www.goodreads.com/quotes/6946-not-all-of-us-can-do-great-things-but-we

23. Accidental Creative. "Finding Your Sweet Spot." Todd Henry. https://www.accidentalcreative.com/creating/why-you-need-tour-sweet-spot/

24. Townsend, John *Leading from Your Gut.* Zondervan: 2018.

25. Buechner, Frederick. *Wishful Thinking* (New York: Harper & Row, 1973), 118-119.

26. https://www.independent.co.uk/news/world/americas/america-new-zealand-and-canada-top-list-of-world-s-most-generous-nations-a6849221.html

27. "Highlights: An overview of giving in 2017," Giving USA 2018.

28. Alix Spiegel, "Why Do We Give? Not Why Or How You Think," npr.com, November 25, 2011.

29. Spiegel.

30. Spiegel.

31. Spiegel.

32. Phyllis Korkki, "Why do people donate to charity?" *The New York Times,* December 22, 2013.

33. Michael Sanders and Francesca Tamma, "The science behind why people give to charity." *The Guardian,* US edition, March 23, 2015.

34. Sanders and Tamma.

35. Sanders and Tamma.

36. https://www.networkforgood.com/nonprofitblog/how-to-get-donations-14-reasons-why-people-donate/

37. Swindoll, Charles. https://www.brainyquote.com/quotes/charles_r_swindoll_578725

38. Gates, Bill. https://www.brainyquote.com/quotes/bill_gates_626084

Made in the
USA
Lexington, KY